LUCAS EDHOLM

Starting a Business

*The Complete Guide to Planning, Launching, and
Boosting the Success of Your Enterprise*

Contents

I

Book 1: Thinking Like an Entrepreneur

1

The Business Mindset

The first step towards becoming a successful entrepreneur is possessing the right mindset. While often overlooked, this aspect is fundamental, and I am speaking based on my personal experience and that of many successful people I know.

Have you ever entertained the thought of starting your own business? If you were not successful so far, or you didn't even dare to try, ask yourself why. It may be that something is wrong with your approach. There are some additional hidden obstacles that you haven't factored into the equation and are preventing you from unleashing your full potential. **I will show you that what is holding you back resides in your own mind.**

In the later sections of this book, you will find plenty of technical advice on how to start and run a business, as well as tips on how to make it long-lasting and profitable. Unfortunately, technical expertise is useless if it is not supported by the right mindset. Why? Because your actions are not just the result of conscious decisions and carefully thought-out plans. Most of your behaviors are driven by habits and deep-set ideas that live in your subconscious. Therefore, unless you radically change your mindset, you won't change the outcome of your performances, regardless of the amount of specific knowledge you acquire.

This truth is self-evident in other aspects of our life that have nothing to do with business. For instance, suppose that you are trying to lose weight. You know that you should stay away from ice cream and cheeseburgers, but will your actions be consistent with your thoughts? After all, you can feel how badly your body craves that junk food, which is what you have been devouring every single day for the past ten years. You can exercise restraint and fight against your instincts. But will you win that battle? The outcome is far from certain. As soon as you relax a bit, you risk relapsing into your previous negative behaviors. It is no mystery that the most successful diets are those that directly target your unhealthy relationship with food and aim at creating new healthier eating habits. Learning every detail about calorie consumption and nutritional values doesn't really help unless it is accompanied by a radical change in your attitude and habits regarding food.

Back to our original question: why are you having such a hard time being successful with your business projects or even finding the resolution to start them? Because in the same way in which your taste for fats and sugars, together with your bad habits, lead you to junk food, your behaviors are guided by negative beliefs that reside in your subconscious. These beliefs are the result of environmental influences, and you may even be totally unaware of having them.

Unless you change those core beliefs, you won't achieve long-lasting results. You may try to act on your newly acquired technical knowledge, enforcing its teachings by sheer willpower. However, if you haven't changed your mindset, you will constantly be fighting against your impulses, like a starving person in front of a hot dog stand.

There is a high chance that, deep in your subconscious mind, there are negative ideas that are influencing your actions. They tell you that it is useless even to try since it is impossible that you will succeed. If you don't get rid of those beliefs, you will always fall short of your ambitions. **Building the right mindset for success is the goal of this section of the book.**

2

The Core Beliefs that Are Holding You Back

What are core beliefs? They are deeply ingrained ideas about yourself, other people, and the world in general, which govern the way you think and act. Being buried in your subconscious, you are often completely unaware of them.

Core beliefs are the result of what you absorbed from your parents and other significant people in your life, as well as from your other life experiences. For most core beliefs, especially those formed during childhood, you never actively choose to believe in them. They were simply planted in your mind through the constant repetition of certain messages.

As a child, you didn't have the mental capacity to evaluate the core beliefs that you were developing and to assess whether you wanted them or not. Now it's different. You are an adult and therefore have the tools to look inside yourself and become aware of the core beliefs that are driving your behaviors.

Some core beliefs are positive and make your life easier. *Here we are concerned with exposing the negative ones, especially those that are preventing you from being successful as an entrepreneur.* The following list describes the most common ones.

Negative Core Belief #1: The majority counts.

You keep hearing that most businesses aren't successful. A whopping 95% of them fail after just a few years. These numbers are real. You might not have realized it yet, but *these statistics about what happens to the "average" and the "majority" have become one of the main reasons why you are giving up without even trying.*

You are driven by your deep-set belief that you can't escape the fate of the majority. Are you still asking questions like the following?

- Why shouldn't those data apply to me?
- How come I should be able to perform differently?
- Are you saying that I'm special, that I'm better than my peers?

Such questions just prove how difficult it is to eradicate the belief that "the majority counts." Unfortunately, most people succumb to the influence of society and never develop the right mindset to succeed. *You can be part of the successful minority, and you will be if only you reset your core beliefs.*

Negative Core Belief #2: Fear of criticism.

Have you ever abandoned or changed your plans because you were afraid of what other people might have thought or said? Maybe even now, you have some business ideas, but you don't feel so confident. You are reluctant to talk about them, even to your friends or family members, because you cannot imagine how they will react. Will they say you are crazy, arrogant, and delusional? Will they be angry, amused, or scornful? You probably don't

6

even want to know. Whatever reaction they will display, there is a high chance that they won't share your enthusiasm and that you won't get the support you wish.

It is very common, especially among young people, to be deep inside afraid of success. Your mind wonders what will happen in case your business takes off and you start making money. How will that be seen in your community? What will your family members or friends say? Will they envy you? Will they change their attitude towards you? Or, even worse, will they blame you and despise you for your accomplishments?

You probably wish you could find a way to be successful without stepping on anyone's toes. You wish you could run ahead, but discreetly, without making others feel as if they have been left behind. It is painful for you to cause envy or resentment in your friends, family members, or other people that are close to you. You are afraid that they won't share your ambitions and that they won't understand or support your projects.

It's time to let go. I am not suggesting letting go of your friends, of course. But you should definitely disregard their opinions. And I mean, disregard them completely. Don't argue, don't try to explain, and don't justify yourself.

Whatever you achieve in life, there will be someone ready to criticize you, someone who doesn't understand you, and someone who opposes you. So what! If you had to wait for unanimous approval before you act, you would never move a finger in your life.

Stop and look inside yourself. Become aware of your instinctive need for approval and fear of other people's judgment. Such feelings are common and, in a sense, even natural. But are they conducive to your goals? No, they aren't and, therefore, must be abandoned.

Consider how much this fear of criticism has been an obstacle to you so far, even if you were not fully aware of it. But how can you give it up? Here are two simple steps you should implement right now:

- Accept the fact that the people with whom you interact have probably been subjected to the same sort of negative messages that are affecting you and getting in the way of your success. So, by listening to them and trying to modify your behavior to appease their minds, you are just giving in to the environment that has been holding you back until now.
- Change your behavior. Stop justifying your choices and trying to get people on your side. Never offer excuses for the actions that you believe are necessary to accomplish your goals. Remember the old saying: *Success requires no apologies.*

Negative Core Belief #3: Fear of failing.

More than success, people tend to fear failure. What if your attempt to start a new business doesn't pan out? How will you justify that with your parents or with your friends, who were skeptical from the very beginning? Will you have proved them right?

The education we receive is not very helpful on this point. We are always taught that there are right answers and wrong answers. In school, we are praised for giving a correct solution, and we are penalized for giving a wrong answer. The message we get is that *mistakes are bad.* They are unacceptable. When we fail a test, we are told that we should have studied more and prepared ourselves better *before* the test.

Unfortunately, the real world doesn't work like that. Most times, you can't know in advance whether a business idea will work, especially if it is extremely original. Read the biographies of the most successful men and women. They failed many times before finally achieving their goals. *The only people who never fail are those who never try.*

Our experience with school and education is responsible for making us so afraid of failing. How can we change it?

- Learn not to be defeated by setbacks. Be persistent in pursuing your goal. Keep your desire alive, reminding yourself of what you are trying to achieve. Say out loud what your motivations and long-term goals are.
- Learn from your mistakes. Successful people reached their goals because they were able to profit from their failures.
- Adopt the same unapologetic attitude we described for negative core belief #2. That is, don't justify yourself with other people. There is no need to do so. Don't make excuses, and don't try to find explanations for your false steps. It's useless and unnecessary.

Negative Core Belief #4: Uneasiness in going against your parents.

You are probably still talking to your parents about your life and future projects. Deep inside, you recognize that they are not competent enough to understand or evaluate your plans. Still, they are your parents, so you feel it is your duty to discuss with them whatever enterprise you want to undertake and seek their approval.

Respecting your family is a fundamental value. However, when listening to your parents' opinions, it is important to recognize their limits. Remember the following:

- Parents tend to protect their children. They will naturally try to dissuade you from any enterprise that they consider too risky.
- Your parents constantly worry about your physical, psychological, and

economic well-being. Therefore, they will always recommend the safest choice. Playing it too safe will preclude you from the possibility of making mistakes, which we have seen above is a fundamental part of the learning process.

- Your parents likely have their own ideas on how your future should be. That prevents them from fully accepting your life choices and being truly supportive. The independent projects you are pursuing might go against what they had envisioned for you.

- They grew up in different times and developed a different set of skills in their youth. In particular, they didn't have the same access to information as you, not having internet, smartphones, or laptops. Hence it might be unreasonable to expect that they will understand your business project, especially if it involves some online activity. Be prepared to experience a certain amount of frustration if you try to explain your ideas to them.

- They might also be a little envious, not finding it fair that you earn money with something that they probably don't even consider a "real job." Perhaps, according to their personal experience, the only way to earn money is through long hours of physical labor. They might be highly suspicious of an online enterprise. Don't let yourself be affected by their misgivings.

You cannot change your parents. You must love them for who they are and accept that they are the product of their times. Be kind and respectful towards them, but at the same time, don't let their attitudes get in the way of your ambition. Here are the most important steps to overcome this negative core belief:

- Leave your parents' house. It will be impossible for you to set your own rules and disregard their judgment if you live under their roof.
- Recognize and accept your parents' limits. Don't blame them for their shortcomings, and don't let a divergence of opinion become a reason for conflict.

- Be ready to proceed with your plans without your parents' approval. It will come eventually, but maybe not now.
- Be always modest, don't try to prove them wrong. Simply do what is right for you.

Negative Core Belief #5: Successful people were blessed with uncommon good luck.

While you are ready to recognize the merits and achievements of successful people, deep inside, you also think that at some point in their path, they enjoyed the benefit of especially favorable circumstances. And what are the chances that such positive factors will favor you in the same way? Very low, you may think. You can work as hard as they did - you tell yourself - but the fact that you haven't had the same success is due more to your lack of good fortune than anything else.

This idea is very appealing to your mind since it takes responsibility away from you. If such a core belief is ingrained in your subconscious, then you can clearly see where your actions will lead you: nowhere. You will never be motivated to act. Instead, you are just passively waiting for something to happen without truly believing that such a lucky circumstance will ever present itself to you.

Ask yourself honestly whether you have even unconsciously been making excuses for your laziness, whether you have somehow gotten comfortable with procrastinating the realization of your plans indefinitely, waiting for the "right moment." Nothing will ever change if you don't act and make that change happen.

We often call luck a cause that we cannot identify. Pick any person you know or have heard of who has achieved great personal and economic success.

Are you sure that you have done everything they did, that you have tried everything they tried? If not, how can you even say they have been luckier than you? We have no clear idea of how many wrong turns they took before finding their way. Even fortunes that seem to have appeared overnight have a long history behind them. There might be years and years of work, failures, and hardships behind a single day of final success. All we see is that day of triumph. We are tempted to call it luck without realizing that it is just the tip of the iceberg. We focus on the moment in which these successful people are reaping the harvest while ignoring the long time during which they have been busy preparing the soil.

Even episodes of genuine good luck, for instance, meeting the right person who helps you grow your business, are not simply due to random chance. On the contrary, they are the result of trying hard enough and for long enough. *Do not wait for opportunities to come your way; instead, go ahead and create your own.* Be resilient and make your own luck as many successful men and women did before you. Ultimately, you will be the main author of your success story.

Negative Core Belief #6: You are not qualified enough.

It is beneficial and rewarding to keep learning and expanding your knowledge throughout your life. But remember that there are many different ways to learn, and the school and university system is only one of them (and often a very inefficient one). If you think you may benefit from additional "formal education," then you should definitely go ahead, take classes, and pursue the degree that you wish to obtain. But first, consider your situation carefully. Ask yourself whether that title is really needed. If you want to be a doctor or a lawyer, then the question is settled. You have a clear path to follow without any concrete alternative. But if your goal is to start a successful business, then you should think a little longer.

Many people believe that before you start a business, you need to get the appropriate titles in the same way in which you need a law degree before you can practice as a lawyer. That is not how it works. Keep the following in mind:

- A lot of the most successful people in business never completed a college degree. Are they uneducated? Not at all. On the contrary, they are extremely knowledgeable. They just took their education into their own hands. They kept an open mind and managed to learn at the right moment whatever was needed to achieve their goals.

- There is another, arguably more important, ability, which is *knowing what not to learn*. While good ideas are rare and valuable (and you must supply them yourself), technical knowledge is extremely cheap. If you don't believe me, just look up the salary of the researchers at the nearest university. Whenever additional technical expertise is required to progress on your project, consider hiring external help.

- In hiring, don't be fooled by titles. Remember that they are not a substitute for actual competencies.

- Don't be afraid of technical knowledge. When you really believe in your project, you must do whatever it takes to bring it to life. If you feel that you need to know more about a certain subject, think twice before wasting time with college classes. Is there any faster or cheaper way to obtain the knowledge you need? Remember that *at the beginning of an enterprise, your time is your greater asset, and you shouldn't waste a second of it.*

- When we take classes, either in school or in college, we expect our teachers to certify through tests and exams that we have succeeded in acquiring the required knowledge. You need to get out of that comfort zone and learn to become the ultimate judge of yourself. Do you know enough about that topic? How can you improve further, and is it really necessary? Only you can tell. Take full responsibility for your competence and skills.

In conclusion, pursue knowledge as needed, but don't be held back by a lack of titles. Don't be afraid to fly high and skip steps. There is a precise hierarchy to climb in the academic or corporate world, but there is no such thing in the business world.

Negative Core Belief #7: You don't deserve to be successful.

You probably appreciate the stories of successful men and women entrepreneurs but perceive them as distant and not something you will ever be able to replicate. After all, you come from a simple family and believe you have no special talent. You are pretty sure that *you don't deserve it.* I have already said this before, but I'll repeat it once more: as long as you feel average, that is all you will be.

What is holding you back has nothing to do with your humble beginnings or starting off with little means. Those factors never prevent people from achieving success. Rather *your main disadvantage consists in having been raised in an environment with a limited mindset, where nobody truly believed that success was obtainable.* You have probably taken on a resigned attitude, which

- Makes you see every obstacle as insurmountable.
- Tells you that you have an assigned position in society.
- Makes you believe that prosperity equals excess and doesn't belong to you.

Having grown up in an environment where those ideas were widespread makes it extremely difficult for you now to imagine yourself as a person of success.

We grow up believing that successful people are somehow "made different" and that they have some special features that "justify" their achievements. That is not true at all. They are people like you and me. Here is the truth: *a negative mindset is the only thing that prevents you from identifying with them.*

Negative Core Belief #8: You shouldn't change.

How often have you heard sentences like "Don't forget where you come from" or "What happened to you? Are you not the same anymore?" They are signs of a widespread belief that one shouldn't change or that one shouldn't even want to change. Has any of your family members or friends ever told you that success will corrupt you and will change you for the worse? They mean well, but they are wrong, and this negative idea is preventing you from realizing your ambitions.

Think of how you were one, two, or ten years ago. If you haven't made tangible progress toward a definite goal, then you should be seriously worried. Are you still stuck in the same routine? That is not a positive sign. Our time on this planet is limited, and we should make every single day count.

It is a blessing in life to be surrounded by a caring partner, supportive friends, and family members who love us unconditionally regardless of our shortcomings. However, we must be careful not to get too comfortable. We shouldn't let the safety and ease of our current situation prevent us from moving forward. My mother often reminds me that I will always find a bed and a meal at her house. I am grateful for that. But I also remember how hard it was for her to let me go when I moved out to go live on my own. At that time, she took it like a betrayal, especially because I was working just a few blocks away from the family house. Remember that *the people around us often see only the benefits of the current situation and cannot understand our non-negotiable needs to progress and change.*

Whatever changes you make to yourself might be uncomfortable or hard to accept for the people who are close to you. Any person who has ever shown up at a family meeting with an unexpected new haircut knows exactly what I am talking about. But the same is true for your personality traits and habits. Suddenly your new job doesn't allow you to hang out with your friends on

Saturday night as you have been doing for years. How will your friends feel about it? The truth is that whenever you change something in your life, the people around you will have to make some changes too, and that may be hard for them. I remember how upset my grandma got with me when I was seventeen. I had just started a new diet and therefore was refusing the food she had prepared with so much love. She didn't take it well. *Accept that you might be hurting people's feelings when you change.* There is nothing you can do about it. If they love you, they will understand eventually.

Change is necessary. If you haven't reached your goals so far, then something in your attitude, personality, or behavior needs to be transformed. *You can't achieve different results if you keep everything the same.*

One of the first things you might want to change is the amount of time you dedicate to others and attending to their needs. That is all time and effort taken away from your own endeavors. Remember that you will be in a better position to help others once you have reached your goals.

Stop saying "yes" to everyone. Saying "no" is not rudeness but self-respect.

Negative Core Belief #9: Wanting more money is morally reprehensible.

You probably think that it is appropriate and desirable to earn enough money to support your family and lead a decent life. At the same time, you may also consider everything more than that as somehow not morally justifiable, just a sign of greed and excess.

We live in a society that normalizes poverty. Actually, it is even worse: scarcity and hardships are often celebrated and presented as the only morally correct alternative. Many religious authorities, community leaders, authors, motivational speakers, and politicians, they all tell you that to find true happiness, you should suppress your desires, not wish for more, detach yourself from material possessions, and pursue a minimalist lifestyle. Their message is: "Be satisfied with the little you have. Don't be obsessed with money, but try to find reward in the effort itself because working hard is noble and pure."

You are also constantly reminded of your privilege of being a first-world citizen. There are people enduring far worse conditions than you: they earn less, live a shorter life, and sometimes even lack basic goods such as food and water. Given this situation, isn't it arrogant for you to ask for more instead of being content with what you already have? Even if you are on welfare or you are just scraping by with a job that only pays a few hundred dollars per month, they will tell you to look at the positive side: you are still better off than the billions of people who are completely destitute. Try to find joy and fulfillment in the life you already live – they'll say – and maybe, if you work hard enough, your employer or the government will even throw a few extra dollars in your direction.

I will now explain once and for all why such arguments are wrong and misguided and why becoming rich and successful is instead a positive and moral pursuit that will bring out the best of your personality. But first, let me stress that *the ideas of scarcity described above are incredibly poisonous to the mind.* If your plan is to start a business and be financially accomplished, **you need to stop being exposed to those negative messages**. And I mean, stop it completely. Avoid people with that scarcity-oriented mindset and turn off the TV. This is a prerequisite to start reprogramming your mind for success by installing new positive core beliefs. The next chapter will discuss in detail the steps through which a new mindset can be achieved.

But now, back to our question: Is pursuing money worth the effort? Will it just set you on the path to unhappiness, as many people claim? It is possible for you to become rich and successful, but why should you want it? Of course, money can buy you the luxury sports car or the lavish holiday you have always dreamed of. That by itself may not make you happy, and you might even dismiss it as unnecessary. But here is something far more important: freedom.

Wealth buys you freedom. Imagine not having to wake up at 7 am to go to work, not having to waste time waiting in commuter traffic, or working a job that doesn't fulfill you. Imagine not having to be subservient to your boss and your superiors, hoping for a slightly higher paycheck. When you have plenty of money, **you will finally be the owner of your time**. You will decide where you want to be and at what time. You will be able to cultivate your passions and hobbies. More importantly, you will be in a position to provide for your family and friends. Trust me, there is no better feeling than being able to donate, especially if we have a personal connection to the person to whom we are giving. Rich people are generous because they can afford to be generous.

When you must constantly worry about surviving until the end of the month, you don't have either the time or the means to be generous. Money problems make you cranky, bitter, and resentful. You are definitely not showing the best side of yourself. It is well known that money issues are among the primary causes of divorce and conflict within a family. That is why **you owe it to yourself and to the people around you to pursue financial freedom.**

Being financially free means being able to make everyday decisions without having to worry about their financial impact. It means that you won't feel your stomach tighten when your child asks you to order pizza, and you are mentally trying to figure out if that is compatible with the family budget. When you are financially free, you are in control of your finances instead of being controlled by them. Think about how many of your decisions are dictated by a worry about money. Did you settle for a regular coffee instead of a latte this morning in order to save that extra dollar? Is that also the reason why you gave up the guacamole in your burrito? That's a pretty sad way of living your life. I am not saying that you should spend recklessly.

But those renounces should just be seen as temporary and not accepted as normal. Aim for something different. Train yourself to want more. Crave financial independence and fight for it, keeping it clear in your mind as your declared goal.

I am sure you dislike living your life in that way. You are also probably affected by much more serious financial concerns. Will you ever be able to retire? Will you be able to provide proper education and medical care to your children? These are not issues that can be dismissed as easily as your craving for a caramel latte.

What can you do about it? You can try and suppress your desires and aspirations and live the life of scarcity advocated by many. Alternatively, you can give free rein to your wishes and *make it imperative for you to find the means to satisfy them.* Don't give up on your desires but instead fuel them and cherish them. They will be the primary force driving your actions. **Foster a yearning for financial independence.**

Having your own business is the best way to move forward toward financial independence. While employees are limited by the salary offered by their employers, the activity of an entrepreneur is open-ended. There is no fixed limit to what you can achieve when you run your business while cultivating a mindset of abundance.

So far, we have seen two important aspects.

1. Having plenty of money allows you to lead a more satisfactory and overall happier life, the main advantage being financial freedom.
2. Being rich and successful brings out the best part of you. It allows you to be generous and cultivate better interpersonal relationships without the weight of financial worries.

I will now argue that *seeking money and riches is also ethical* (unless you are planning to rob a bank, of course, but here we are obviously talking about legitimate enterprises). I will show you how *in pursuing your financial success, you are also benefiting society.* This runs contrary to the widespread false belief that you can make money only at the expense of someone else.

What is money? It is just a convenient way of exchanging and transferring wealth, a way of keeping track of debits and credits. Money is not an evil creation of modern times. The concept is instead embedded in the social nature of humans. Without a way of keeping track of debits and credits, nobody would do anything for others, and collaboration among people who don't share family ties would be impossible to manage. Consider all the products and devices that you use in your everyday life. Each of them is the result of the combined efforts of dozens, if not hundreds, of people with different expertise. Money is what regulates the interactions among all those people and enables them to profit from working together towards a common goal.

When you buy a milkshake for $2, it means that at that specific time and place, you think you are better off with that milkshake in your hand rather than the $2 in your pocket. Similarly, whenever someone pays for a product or a service you sell, they feel that your product has more value for them than the money they are exchanging for it. If you make a lot of money, it means that you have created a lot of value for society. The money you earn is just a way for society to say, "I owe you," a measure of the credit you have accumulated with the public.

By making money, you are producing value for society. The money game is ultimately a wealth-creation game.

Politicians almost never talk about creation and instead love talking about *distribution.* They discuss distributing resources, money, and jobs. The underlying assumption is that there is only a limited amount of wealth and a finite number of jobs, and the only question is their distribution, over which, of course, they have a strong influence. This narrative suits their interests. It takes responsibility away from you while magnifying their role, presenting them as saviors. Trusting them – they say – is your only hope to "receive your fair share."

Don't wait for someone to hand you a bigger slice of the cake. Instead, go ahead and bake your own! Clearly, things are very different from what politicians claim. There isn't a limited amount of wealth or a finite number of jobs in the world. One just has to look at history to find proof of this statement. I bet you would prefer to be a poor American today than an aristocrat in 18th-century France. Even if you live very modestly, you can probably enjoy the use of a cell phone and a TV, and you can afford to eat meat every day. You definitely live a longer and more satisfying life than any rich person from three hundred years ago. What has happened since then? Did politicians devise a better way of distributing resources? Not at all. Simply, the total amount of wealth has increased dramatically. You may still have a small slice, but it has been cut from an astronomically bigger cake.

How many times have you heard that "money is the root of all evil"? This common negative connotation is due to the fact that making money is seen as a greedy accumulation. It is believed that rich people hoard a resource that is finite. As we have seen, this is not the case: they have money because they have produced a great amount of wealth, creating value for society, which in turn owes them a lot.

In game theory, a situation is said to be zero-sum if one person's gain is equivalent to another person's loss, and therefore there is effectively no net change in overall wealth. **The money game is not a zero-sum game.** It is a *wealth creation game*, not one of distribution. It is a game of abundance. For you to get richer, there doesn't need to be someone somewhere else in the world who gets poorer. You are creating something new, producing new wealth, not taking away from others. In many cases, the exact opposite happens. When a business grows and becomes structured, many people, besides the person who started it, will profit from it.

Of course, creating a prosperous business is tough, and there is competition. But the point I am making here is that, for your company to be successful, it must provide some added value to consumers and to society at large. The money you make is a measure of your ability to produce that value.

Every form of competition involving status, instead, is a zero-sum game. Playing a *status game* means trying to be the first in some hierarchy and have your standing acknowledged by others. Politics is an example of a zero-sum game. When a politician is elected, some other is not. One wins, and another one loses. In that game, people are competing for a limited number of seats.

We play status games very often throughout our life. During childhood, I would say that we did little else except for playing status games. We want to be the most popular in our group of friends, the fastest in the school run, or the first to show up with the newest model of shoes. In a sense, we are genetically programmed for this type of competition since they have been the basis of the organization of societies for thousands of years. When humans were hunter-gatherers, storing and accumulating wealth was almost impossible, and therefore the safest way to guarantee your future was to try and earn high status. People would focus their efforts on securing a high position in the social hierarchy.

We still see people playing for status all around us, even though the game doesn't have the high prizes it had in prehistoric times. Everyone nowadays tries to achieve popularity by gathering followers and likes on social media. What do they get in return for their frantic efforts? Most often, nothing since nothing of value has been produced. As the old saying goes, *play stupid games, win stupid prices.*

If you want to grow a successful business and pursue financial independence, you must stay away from status games. You should play the money game instead, which, as we have discussed above, involves a completely different set of rules. It is a game of creation, cooperation, and abundance.

When someone says that money is bad, that being wealthy is immoral, or that there is value in being poor, they are just virtue signaling and bidding for status. They are trying to score points by putting down builders of wealth like you. Remember that the status game they are playing is zero-sum, and they can only emerge at someone else's expense.

Sometimes I accidentally come across a book or website advocating "a simpler minimalist lifestyle not based on money." One of the most common reasons given to pursue this lifestyle is that "people will respect you for it." Such a sentence gives away that what they are proposing is essentially a status game. They are asking you to give up your pursuit of wealth in order to gain the recognition and approval of others. It is up to you whether you want to engage in a futile fight for status or direct your energy towards a more productive endeavor and play the money game instead.

Negative Core Belief #10: You should stay on the path you have started.

You have been led to believe that there is a clear path to follow in life: go to school, learn some technical skills in a certain field, and finally, try to secure the best-paying job you can find that requires those skills. This is the standard recipe promoted by society, and at first glance, it seems to provide a clear and safe way to move forward. The problem with this track is that it won't lead you to the most desirable goal, which is financial independence.

Imagine that your life is a trip up a mountain. Unfortunately, you have started to follow a path blindly without asking where it will bring you. It is not your fault; that is what happens to everyone. Now that you have finally opened your eyes, you can see that walking that track will only get you halfway to the top. However, you have already invested so much of your energy in climbing along that way. What are you going to do? Will you just spend the rest of your life down there looking up at the people who made it to the top and envying them? Those people, of course, are those who have reached financial independence. The track of "study, learn some skills, find a job," which you started years ago, will never bring you there. Again, what will you do?

It is normal and understandable that you feel reluctant to go back down to the bottom of the mountain and look for another way up. But keep in mind that the descent might actually be the most difficult part. While the feelings of frustration and defeat in retracing your steps can be overwhelming, you will find new motivation and confidence once you have started the new, more direct path to the top. That path is given by an entrepreneurial mindset properly programmed for success.

Here is another interesting example that can serve as a metaphor for your situation. In Asia, people used to capture monkeys by putting some fruits and nuts inside a small hole in a tree. The opening had to be just wide enough for the monkey to fit its arm inside. In that way, after grabbing the food, the monkey was unable to take its clenched fist out of the hole. Amazingly enough, even when approached by hunters, the monkey was unwilling to let go of its prize. Rather than abandon the nuts, it would remain trapped, risking its freedom and its life.

Aren't we all a bit like the monkey, naturally reluctant to let go of our salary, our childhood friends, and our old beliefs?

Have you fallen for the few nuts that society has given you? It is comforting to hold on to what we have (or believe we have). Unfortunately, as was the case for the monkey, unwillingness to let go comes at a very high price: you are missing out on freedom. You are never in the position to look around, to seek another more profitable and more successful path.

You keep holding on to the little you have, not understanding that you can aspire to much more and start pursuing something different. But first, it is crucial that you find the resolution to open that fist and let go of what you are holding now. You will have relapses; you will start questioning yourself. *What am I doing? Am I mad? This is too risky.* At the first misstep in the new path, you will doubt the entire enterprise. But it is crucial that you persist.

Getting rid of negative core beliefs and reframing your attitude for success are not easy tasks. The next chapter will provide more details on how they can be achieved. In the meantime, here are three important takeaways from this chapter:

1. **Remember that the majority is not relevant**. You may not realize it, but your subconscious mind reasons in terms of what happens to the majority because those are the data it has been fed through the years. Your mindset and judgment are based on what happened to "the others," unconsciously assuming that you won't be able to perform differently. Stop worrying about the average! That is just a statistic and says nothing about the personal story of individuals. Refuse to be another number in the stats.

2. **Limit your exposure to negative messages and look for positive ones instead**. Seek out the outliers, those who have succeeded. Look for them in your family, in your community, or online, and let yourself be inspired. Reason on the success stories you witness around you. Why was that restaurant so successful while many others in the same neighborhood failed? Why did Alexis get that job among hundreds of applicants? Always pay special attention to the successful minority, on the local as well as on the global scale. You must see yourself as part of that group. Whatever business or activity you wish to undertake, you will find plenty of positive examples of success from which you can gain knowledge and inspiration.

3. **Create in your mind a vivid image of yourself in the position you want to obtain**. Close your eyes and focus on your goals. See yourself as

having already achieved those goals. You want to build a clear image for your mind, something that will stick and will work as a light in front of your eyes, guiding your actions toward success.

3

Reprogramming Your Mind for Entrepreneurial Success

In the last chapter, we have described some common negative core beliefs that may be preventing you from progressing in your life and achieving your goals. Be honest with yourself. Do you share any of those beliefs? Can you think of other negative beliefs that are getting in your way? It is important that you expose those insidious deep-set ideas and become aware of the ways in which they are influencing your behavior.

Maybe you are reluctant to admit having those beliefs. I can imagine you feeling indignant while reading the previous chapter and saying to yourself, "Afraid of criticism? Me? I definitely don't care about other people's opinions". But your conscious mind is not very reliable in these judgments. Remember that we are trying to uncover convictions that are deeply buried in your subconscious. Consider your performance and the results you have achieved (or not achieved) so far. *If your behaviors are consistent with those false beliefs, then there is little doubt that they are there in the background driving your actions.*

How to get rid of those false beliefs?

Unfortunately, *it is not enough to combat them with rational arguments.* How many times do our behaviors not match our words? For instance, if you smoke cigarettes, you are perfectly aware of the negative consequences on your health. Both smokers and non-smokers share the same knowledge in their conscious minds. What is different, then? Addiction and habit have created in the smoker some unconscious negative core beliefs, such as

- Smoking is cool.
- Smoking is socially acceptable.
- Smoking is satisfying.
- Smoking helps me control my anxiety.

While a smoker and a non-smoker can rationally agree on the negative effects of cigarettes, their difference in behavior is determined by a difference in their subconscious beliefs.

Can you make a smoker quit simply by pointing out the damage to his lungs? Of course not. In the same way, to give up some core beliefs, we can't just reason over the negative outcomes that they produce in our lives. How do we do it, then?

Before we answer, we need to examine the way in which core beliefs and behaviors are related. In particular, we need to understand how **our core beliefs are reinforced by the very actions they determine**. Let me give you an example. Suppose you harbor in your subconscious the conviction, "I am useless." Now, because of that subconscious idea, you are less willing to act or try new and different paths since, deep inside, you are already convinced that you will fail. This inertia will prevent you from achieving any goals, thus reinforcing the belief that you are useless. But it was that belief that made you not act in the first place!

To eliminate a negative core belief, you need to break that vicious circle. There are two ways to do that, and you should pursue them at the same time.

28

1. **Change behavior.** Use your willpower to act differently in a way that is consistent with the new positive beliefs you want to fix in your mind. It will feel unnatural at first, but don't give up: *this is an essential step to interrupt the self-reinforcement that the negative core beliefs are receiving from your current behaviors.* The longer you keep up the new positive pattern, day after day, the more it will influence your subconscious. Remember that the negative core beliefs were themselves established by repetition. You are just using the same strategy to install the new positive ones.

2. **Work on your mind.** We have seen how the mind is especially susceptible to images. Therefore, to influence it, *you must create a vivid image of the new self to which you are aiming.* Let me give you a concrete example. Suppose that you have a bad habit of biting your nails. How do you give it up? One strategy is to plant into your mind an image of yourself as a person with manicured hands and nicely trimmed nails. Focus your attention on that image several times every day. Biting your nails is not consistent with this new image of yourself. Therefore, with time, you will elicit a phenomenon known as *cognitive dissonance*: a clash between your beliefs and your actions. If you hold on tightly to the image that you have grown in your mind, you will be inclined to change your behaviors to adapt to it.

To sum up, for each negative core belief you have identified in yourself, find

1. **Some behaviors contradict that belief**. Pursue those behaviors using your willpower.
2. **A new image of yourself based on the opposite positive belief**. Conjure this image to your mind as often as possible so that it will stick.

Here is an example of positive beliefs that should replace the negative ones described in the previous chapter.

Positive Core Belief #1: I am part of the successful minority. The fate of the majority doesn't concern me. My strong desires, backed by definite plans and determination, will lead me to achieve my goals.

Positive Core Belief #2: I won't be influenced by what other people think or say.

Positive Core Belief #3: I am not afraid of failing. I am ready to face any setback and to learn from my mistakes.

Positive Core Belief #4: I will not let the love I feel toward my parents and family members cloud my judgment.

Positive Core Belief #5: I will not wait passively for a stroke of luck but will create my own opportunities for success.

Positive Core Belief #6: Ignorance is a choice. I am willing to educate myself in the most efficient possible way in whatever matter is needed to achieve my goals.

Positive Core Belief #7: I deserve to be happy, successful, and rich.

Positive Core Belief #8: I am aware that progress involves changing, and I am ready to embrace those changes. I will strive to improve myself, my attitude, and my mindset.

Positive Core Belief #9: It is positive and ethical to pursue financial success. I will be producing value for society. Moreover, having more money will make me a better person, enabling me to express my generosity.

Positive Core Belief #10: It is appropriate to give up a path that doesn't lead to my newly set goals, even if it means starting from scratch and having to find a new way. Now that I have a clear goal in front of my eyes, I can and will choose a track that will take me to my destination.

Can you see yourself as a person holding these beliefs and acting according to such principles? Here are some practical tips to help you fix in your mind this new positive image of yourself. Make sure you get back to this list often and keep repeating these exercises. With time, you will see the results in your actions, which will begin to be driven by the new set of principles.

Declare your goals and hold yourself accountable. Always hold yourself to the highest standards. When you declare your financial goal, choose a realistic amount, and write it on a piece of paper together with the date before which you will earn that amount of money. Now close your eyes and focus. Try to see yourself in possession of exactly that amount of money. How does it feel? What will you do with it? How did you earn it? How much of that money will be reinvested in your business, and how? Fill the picture with details and try to feel as if you were truly there. The best way to make an image vivid and make it stick in your mind is to attach some emotions to it. Repeat this exercise for each of your personal and financial goals. Always imagine yourself in the position of success that you want to achieve.

See yourself as a better person who has achieved money and success. How will you express your generosity? What will you do for others, and how will you treat yourself? Feel all the positive emotions associated with the financial independence that you will have earned. Experience the sense of liberation of not having to work a nine-to-five job and living in abundance. This exercise will help fuel a burning desire for success. You must truly want it in order to achieve it.

Rehearse success in your mind using the following mental exercise. Take for granted that the next step of your project has been achieved, and plan further ahead. For instance, let's say your goal is opening a restaurant. Assume that has been achieved, your restaurant is successful and look ahead. Where would you open your second location? And the third? How will you reinvest the money coming in from this business? The best entrepreneurs are those who are fully aware of the present but at the same time projected toward the future. Use this strategy when you are considering your future as a business owner and planning your way to financial success.

Hang out with people who share similar goals and ambitions. Expand your horizons by getting in touch with other entrepreneurs. Share your time and opinions with people who have a positive mindset of abundance. Consider isolating yourself from your parents and your old friends, at least at the beginning of your journey as an entrepreneur. If you keep hearing messages which resonate with the negative core beliefs you are trying to get rid of, it will be impossible to remove them from your mind.

Act in a way that is conducive to your goals. Carefully evaluate each of your actions to understand if they are driven solely by your plans and desires or are still affected by negative core beliefs.

You are an individual with your own skills, strengths, and ambition. You have the potential to succeed in any enterprise you want to undertake. Bad news: there are some negative core beliefs in your unconscious mind. You adopted them in the past without giving a second thought, and unfortunately, they are still affecting your life. Good news: you are now fully aware of the situation, and you can ask, *Are these beliefs working for me or against me? Do they represent the type of person I want to be?* **You can make a conscious effort to change those core beliefs that are not a good fit for you and are not consistent with your goals.**

You owe it to yourself to make those changes. As a result, you will

- Improve the way you feel about yourself.
- Reduce negative thinking.
- Act in a way that is helpful to achieve your goals.

You can perform a similar analysis and use the same strategies to consider all the different aspects of your life, even those not related to financial success.

Proceed exactly as we did above. Evaluate your real-life results objectively and expose the negative core beliefs that are getting in your way, preventing you from reaching your goals. Then use the techniques just described to remove those unfavorable ideas from your unconscious mind. For instance, is it possible that your romantic relationships are also affected in some ways by negative core beliefs picked up in the past?

One important warning: the reprogramming of your mind will be uncomfortable. This is a consequence of the cognitive dissonance that you will experience every time your actions and your inner beliefs do not match. It's normal at this stage.

Comfort derives from acting in harmony with your core beliefs. You feel comfortable when you are behaving in a way that instinctively "feels right" that is consistent with the image you have of yourself. Unfortunately, if that image is plagued by negative beliefs, the attitudes that make you comfortable can be damaging to your personal goals.

Often, the biggest obstacles to success lie in our own minds. The goal of this book was to show you how to eliminate those obstacles and reprogram your mind for success.

How will you understand when you have finally succeeded in reprogramming your mind with new positive core beliefs? *At that point, you will feel different. You will suddenly be inspired by new ideas and energy.* Follow those instincts: it's the new mindset kicking in!

The comfort zone that you have inhabited so far is not your natural place. You didn't choose it; you didn't build it. Your circumstances and past experiences did that for you. Now you have a choice. You can stay in that situation. Alternatively, you can face the discomfort of changing and get ready to finally pursue your personal goals.

4

From Employee to Entrepreneur

Some people had the luck of growing up in a positive environment which helped them develop the right mindset for success. If this is not your case, it is time to take charge of the situation and create your own positive environment, surrounding yourself with the right people and fostering the right ideas in your mind. In the previous chapters, we analyzed the false beliefs that are preventing you from succeeding. We have also described the best strategies to install new positive core beliefs to reprogram your mind for success. This new mindset will enable you to perform in stressful situations and maximize your results.

What kind of results? Well, if you are reading this book, it means that you are interested in entrepreneurship, making money, and reaching financial independence. You have either started your business or wish to do so.

In this section, I will give you a summary of the changes you must make to your approach, highlighting the differences with the employee mindset. What you will read here is a set of instructions, but if you follow the strategies of the previous chapter, these behaviors will soon become automatic. While in the beginning, you will have to make a conscious effort to pursue them, they will gradually become straightforward consequences of your new mindset. At some point, they will constitute your standard approach to your work.

The results you will achieve by operating according to the following principles will surprise you.

Principle #1: Learn as you go. Employees base their professional growth on perfecting some skills without giving too much thought about what those skills will be used for. If you think about it, this is consistent with the standard approach to life we have been taught. We are told to first study and get a degree. You must learn what your professors teach you, and you are not allowed to ask what you will use that for in life. That is simply an unacceptable question. Just focus on learning – they say – and you will find a use for your knowledge at some point in the future.

Entrepreneurs are very different in this respect. They start a project with little input, knowing that no matter how much they study or learn, they will never be fully prepared for what lies ahead. Most often, their path will involve unforeseen difficulties and require skills that they wouldn't have been able to imagine beforehand. Therefore, entrepreneurs don't fall into the perfection trap. They value doing over learning without a fixed and clear goal in mind. They believe in keeping focused on a final objective and learning during the journey.

This is not an easy approach to pursue. We tend to be insecure and feel that we don't know enough or that we are not ready. But will you ever be truly ready? Just remember that the school system is where you have learned your current attitude, and schools are designed to produce perfect employees.

To sum up, employees perfect their skills and seek directions. Entrepreneurs are those who direct, who create a path, and pick up new skills along the way.

Principle #2: Never wait, but instead, create your opportunities. Employees are usually set on a course of action and are unwilling to reconsider. Most of the time, the route hasn't even been decided by them. They are just carefully following a path, acting according to a fixed set of instructions. If circumstances are not favorable, they will wait passively until a new opportunity arises that is consistent with their plans. Very often, this "waiting for the right moment" becomes an excuse to procrastinate indefinitely.

Entrepreneurs, on the other hand, never wait. They are flexible and keep their mind open, looking for new possibilities. When the circumstances are different from those they had foreseen, they don't halt their plans but instead devise a new strategy. They know that with the right mindset, they can succeed and realize their goals regardless of external factors. With this attitude, entrepreneurs can factor luck out of the equation.

Principle #3: Value progress over money. Employees work for money. Their goal is to gain a higher salary as well as a better position in the hierarchy of the company for which they work.

Entrepreneurs don't work for money. They work for their business. Entrepreneurs don't have an hourly rate because there is no price for their time. They simply wouldn't perform a task that is not consistent with their goals, not even in exchange for money. Entrepreneurs have a mission, they get satisfaction from what they create, and their work is always focused on improvement. Good work is that which moves you forward, bringing you closer to your objective. Remember that progress can take many different forms: it may consist in perfecting some skills needed for the business or coming up with new ideas and solutions. But progress is always the goal, not money.

As counter-intuitive as it may sound, entrepreneurs can afford to focus less on money. They are ready to work for months or even years without profits as long as they see sufficient progress. As they believe in generating wealth in the long term, they don't measure short-term success in terms of money.

Principle #4: **Make your frustration temporary**. Employees are stuck day after day in the same boring routine. Combine that with the fact that they are often playing a status game against their colleagues or superiors to ascend the company's hierarchy, and you get a measure of their frustration. Frustration is, for employees, a constant state which sometimes makes them become arrogant or aggressive towards their co-workers or family members.

Entrepreneurs also face frustrating moments. Their problems, however, are temporary. They are used to facing obstacles and, above all, know how to handle failure. They understand that every setback contains the seeds for new, more profitable opportunities. In the worst-case scenario, they are not afraid of starting again from zero with a brand-new plan. And let's not forget the sense of empowerment deriving from playing a wealth creation game as opposed to a zero-sum one.

Principle #5: Fuel your desires. Employees are dreamers. They dream of breaking their unbearable nine-to-five routine, having a lavish lifestyle, buying a new car, taking their family on an expensive holiday, and so on. The problem is that they have no plans whatsoever to make such dreams come true. They don't really believe that they will realize any of them but are instead resigned to keeping them in their fantasy. As a result, they feel guilty even for having such thoughts.

Entrepreneurs, on the other hand, have solid plans to give shape to their dreams. They can afford not to give up on their desires for financial independence and prosperity.

Principle #6: Work smart rather than hard. Employees often feel the need to show that they work as hard as possible. They might need to impress their boss, their colleagues, or maybe just themselves to feel confident that they truly deserve the money they earn. Entrepreneurs, on the other hand, don't care about showing off their diligence and are instead only concerned with results. This is the reason why they prefer to work smartly, maximizing their results with the minimum possible effort.

Principle #7: Don't blame others for your mistakes but instead correct yourself. Employees are often afraid of making mistakes. In fact, they could be blamed for them and lose money. A significant error could even cost them their job. Therefore, when a mistake is made, it is common for employees to try and justify themselves and shift the blame. It is also likely that after one such episode, employees will be more guarded, losing confidence in their abilities.

Entrepreneurs behave differently. They are in a position to take full responsibility for their mistakes. In this way, without having to worry too much about the consequences of what happened, they can assess the situation honestly, analyze what happened, and learn a valuable lesson for the future. Entrepreneurs see failures as new opportunities and don't lose their enthusiasm. After all, progress has been made since a mistake offers the possibility to learn and improve.

Principle #8: Know how to take risks. Employees are attached to the idea of security and are unwilling to take any risk. Entrepreneurs instead know how to evaluate and handle risks. They are aware that "security" often means being resigned to frustration and mediocrity.

This new entrepreneurial mindset is the necessary starting point to make your actions produce results. But what should these actions be? The next part of the book will give you concrete technical guidance to start your business adventure.

II

Book 2: From Idea to Reality

5

Giving Shape to Your Idea

Starting your own business will give a powerful shake to your routine. It will provide you with a sense of purpose, direct your time and efforts toward a concrete goal, and unleash the potential that has remained hidden inside you for so long. Last but not least, it will bring you long-term wealth and prosperity, together with a fulfilling sense of accomplishment.

What is so special about being a business owner? How is it different from working a 9-to-5 job? Here is the main difference: you may be hard-working, talented, knowledgeable, skilled, creative, or a master of your craft. That alone, however, will *not be enough* to make you a successful entrepreneur. Let me explain this point better.

A 9-to-5 job is focused on your skills. Whether you are a chef, a barber, a journalist, a teacher, or an airplane pilot, your technical skill is your most important asset. You are paid because of your proficiency at cooking, cutting hair, writing, teaching classes, or bringing an airplane from one airport to the next. The types of challenges you face every day are of a similar kind, and your goals do not change much from one day to the next. Most likely, you have undergone some period of training, even months or possibly years, to develop and perfect that specific skill.

The job of an entrepreneur is not focused on a specific skill. For instance, let's assume you are the owner of a restaurant. How is that different from being a chef? Well, your task is now "running the restaurant." Let's see what that involves. First, you need to hire the people who are going to cook for your restaurant, as well as the waiters. You must choose what menu you wish to offer, what products to buy, and from where. You have to decide the prices and the opening hours. But you also need to worry about keeping the restaurant clean, engaging with the customers, managing the finances, and dealing with the wholesalers. How are people going to know about your restaurant? You need to take care of the marketing. Do you want to build a website for the restaurant? Will you advertise on social media? Are you going to use a system of online reservations? Will you do delivery? And so on, with a thousand other similar issues. It doesn't sound boring at all, does it?

Being a business owner means focusing more on the process rather than the specific steps. An employee will concentrate on one individual task, like cooking a dish, cleaning the floor, or building a website for the restaurant. Their duty is consistent with their skills and expertise. As a business owner, however, you need to deal with the bigger picture because your ultimate task is making a complex machine work like clockwork. Most of the time, it won't. There will always be difficulties, and every day will bring new and unforeseen challenges. To face them effectively, you need to be flexible, creative, and willing to learn and expand on your knowledge in many different areas. The risks are high, and the responsibilities are high, but the rewards will also be high, both financially and personally.

"Know your enemy," recommends the Chinese general Sun Tzu in his famous book *The Art of War*. To be successful in any enterprise, you first need to have a clear picture of the challenges you are facing. For this reason, it is crucial that you understand the complexities of the task of a business owner before you start that career, especially if you are a first-generation entrepreneur and therefore can't turn to your parents or relatives for advice on how to run a business.

Let me repeat again the message of this chapter: to be a successful business owner. You need to give up the 9-to-5 mentality. Be ready to encounter everyday new and different challenges in areas in which you have received no training at all. Remember that your job is to understand the whole picture.

6

Capital and Credit

Creating a new business involves some initial expenses. The money you must gather to pay those expenses is called **startup capital**. Where are you going to find that money? Well, the most immediate answer is you dip into your pocket or ask your family for help. Unfortunately, neither your pockets nor those of your parents might be deep enough.

Here is a simple thought experiment. Think of anything that is owned by your household and has monetary value. These goods are called **household assets**. They are things like your home and furniture, your car, but also the money in your bank account, and even household items like jewelry and electronics. Now sum together the value of all your household assets and subtract all your debts. You have obtained a quantity frequently mentioned in the media called **family wealth**.

If your savings or those of your family are unavailable, you can always try and get access to **credit**. When a bank extends you credit, it means that you receive money based on the trust that you will pay back your debt in the future. However, banks will demand a certain minimum balance in the account, as well as some **collateral value**, that is, some assets pledged as security for repayment of the loan.

The question that is relevant to us is the following: *Should you try to get a loan from a bank to start your business?* Said otherwise, is it good to rely on credit at the beginning of your business enterprise?

It depends, of course, on the type of business you are trying to start. But I would recommend not taking out a loan on your first business attempt. There are several good reasons for this. First, your loan request might get rejected. If that happens, you will have wasted precious time drafting plans that you now don't have the means to carry out. The second reason why you shouldn't rely on credit is that the bank would then become a stakeholder in your business. Remember that the bank has the right to demand payment in full at their discretion at any time, with or without cause. What if you have already spent the borrowed money to buy equipment, but you have not yet generated any revenue?

Here we need to introduce another important economic concept: **cash flow**. This term refers to the net balance of cash moving into and out of a business at a specific point in time. This shouldn't be confused with **profit**, which instead indicates the amount of money left over after all expenses have been paid. According to data from the U.S. Bureau of Labor Statistics, about 20% of small businesses in the United States fail within the first year. By the end of their fifth year, roughly 50% have faltered. After ten years, only around a third of businesses have survived. Do you want to know the most common cause of failure? A lack of cash flow. Said otherwise, these businesses run out of cash. They might have other material assets, but they lack the money to keep operations going.

There are two important lessons we can learn from these data. The first is that lack of cash flow is already a chronic problem for new businesses. Therefore, why put additional strain on yourself by owing to a bank, which might claim its money back at any time? The second lesson is that, especially if you are undertaking your very first business enterprise, there is a possibility that you will fail. Of course, I don't wish that for you, and you should always stay positive and fight hard for success. But even if your first business attempt doesn't work out, it's no big deal. It is okay to make mistakes, and you will definitely have acquired important experience for the future. However, it is better to fail small. Do you want to have to use the profit from your new business to pay back the loan you took out to start the previous one?

Here is the message of the discussion so far: to move your first steps in the world of entrepreneurship, it is recommended to **start with your own capital, no matter how small**. Taking credit from a bank is not a good option because of the following reasons:

- It might be hard to obtain.
- It will force you to have more cash flow available in case the bank demands full payment.
- There is a chance that your first business attempt won't be successful. In that case, it's better to fail small.

I know what you are thinking now. *What if I don't have enough money? What if my capital is too small?* Well, in that case, you will just have to start out small. Your business will grow bigger in due time. Young entrepreneurs often fall into the trap of wanting to emulate big competitors. It's understandable. You look around you and see corporations with dozens of locations, hundreds of employees, millions of dollars in revenues, and massive and expensive advertising on roadside billboards, on radios, and on TV stations. You naturally ask yourself: *How can I compete with them with my limited resources?*

Remember that those huge corporations were once small, probably much smaller than you imagine. Jeff Bezos started Amazon from in his garage. Colonel Sanders served food from his own dining room table for four years before expanding to six tables and then going on to create what is now the second-largest restaurant chain in the world. I am talking about KFC, of course. Do you know that if you were to eat at a different KFC location every day, it would take you 62 years to visit them all? The largest restaurant chain in the world is McDonald's, which had humble beginnings too. It started in 1940 with a single restaurant in San Bernardino, California. Now in 2021, if you were to visit a different McDonald's location every single day, a lifetime wouldn't be enough to see them all. Indeed, it would take you over 106 years.

It is not a random chance that those success stories sound so similar. They are showing you the most reliable way to succeed: start small, then expand. Trust the process. It must have some merits, after all, if it produced so many billionaires. Besides, it's totally unrealistic to want to enter the market at the same level as those who have already been in the business for many years. You need to watch your competitors closely, look up to them and learn from them, but you must also walk your own path. Think big but act small. Frantically trying to catch up with some big fish while disregarding your own goals will set you up for failure.

We can go even further and ask whether a company actually gains some advantage in starting out small. The answer is a definite YES. Being modest in size means

- being more flexible and therefore able to experiment more.
- being better at absorbing losses since mistakes are made on a smaller scale.

All the companies we mentioned above experienced setbacks and difficulties at the beginning. It took their founders a lot of time and mistakes to find out the most efficient way to realize their business ideas. Richard and Maurice McDonald wanted to push to the extreme the principles of modern fast-food restaurants. Colonel Sanders's goal was to popularize chicken in the fast-food industry, challenging the established dominance of hamburgers. A lot of experimenting was involved in discovering the best course of action to make those ideas concrete and profitable. That long phase of trial and error was possible only because the companies were still small in size. Can you imagine what it would mean to experiment with a different menu every week in dozens or even hundreds of locations at a time? Or enduring a loss on such a gargantuan scale when you are just starting out and haven't yet built any backup? Mistakes are necessary at the beginning of an enterprise; keep them small, and they will help you grow. Keep your company modest in size and flexible until you have found out your way and understood what really works. Only then can you begin to scale up.

Here is the bottom line: **save some money and use it as your startup capital**. If you are starting a brick-and-mortar business, focus your efforts on one single location. If your activity does not require a physical headquarter, start it online. We will discuss in a later chapter the opportunities offered by online markets. Regardless of the type of business you are undertaking, make sure you balance your ambitions with patience. Rome wasn't built in a day. In the same way, big successful companies have a long history behind them: their leaders were able to expand them constantly over the years.

Are you still not convinced that it is not only possible but even beneficial to start with little capital? With a simple online search, you can find many more examples to hammer home the message. Those entrepreneurs might not have had capital at the beginning, but sure enough, they had a vision. **Ideas are worth more than money for someone starting a business**. Those ideas will constitute your true startup capital.

Let us go back to credit. We have discussed why it is not advisable to rely on a line of credit to start your first business. However, you never know what will happen in the years to come. You might experience a moment of financial difficulty, or some investment opportunity may arise requiring you to come up quickly with an important sum of money. For all these reasons, **credit should always be available as an option**. You won't borrow money to start your very first company, but you might want to or have to use this option at some point in the future.

To increase your chances of having access to credit, you need a good **credit score**. You are probably already familiar with the credit score system: each of us is assigned a numerical value that reflects our record in repaying debts.

It is crucial that you understand the importance and urgency of improving your credit score. It needs to be done in advance. You cannot wait to take action until the moment of emergency when you need a loan: then, it will be already too late. **Start repairing or building your credit right now.** First, find a bank that will give you a credit card, and then follow these two simple rules:

1. Pay your bills on time since one of the most important credit-scoring factors is your payment history.
2. Use your credit cards sparingly since another scoring factor is how much of your available credit limits you're currently using (try to stay below 30%).

I hope to have convinced you in this chapter that having little or no capital and limited access to credit does not prevent you from starting a successful business. On the contrary, you can exploit what is sometimes called *the power of being broke*. Starting with scarce resources can be your strength as a new entrepreneur. You will have to come up with the cleverest solutions to your problems, using your modest capital in a creative and efficient way. At the end of the day, this is what a successful business is all about: achieving more with less.

Think of every possible way in which you can save money. For instance, do you really need to pay for advertisement, or can you instead start off promoting your products online for free? Find cheaper and more ingenious solutions than your competitors, who are probably wasting valuable resources stuck in doing what they have been doing for years. One last tip in the same direction: wait as long as possible before hiring new fixed collaborators. Use freelancers if possible. Remember that increase in size will make it harder for you to work on a budget. Moreover, you will lose flexibility. It's easier to maneuver a small team rather than an army.

7

Positioning Your Product or Service

One of your most important tasks as a new entrepreneur is to effectively position your product in the market. What does it mean? Let's consider the following example. Say that you want to sell food. You first need to ask yourself whom you are competing against. Is it the hot dog stand across the street, the local steakhouse, or the Michelin-starred restaurant downtown? This is a crucial question because, depending on the answer, you will be addressing very different types of customers. Let's assume that you will be selling sandwiches and therefore fighting for clients with the hot dog stand. These clients will probably be people in a hurry who want to grab a quick bite during their lunch break or while waiting for the bus. The next question for you is: how does your product compare to the hot dogs sold by the competition? Why should a customer buy a sandwich from you instead? Is it *healthier*? Is it *more customizable*? When you are asking this, what you are doing is **finding a position** for your sandwiches in the landscape of all the possible alternatives offered by the market.

Launching a new product is like entering a battlefield: you need to understand who your enemies are, where your strengths lie, and what kind of battles you are going to fight. Only then can you choose the best spot where to place your artillery. Positioning is like digging your first trench or setting up the generals' headquarters. Every future move will start from there.

51

Indeed, identifying your competitors and the place occupied by your product within the market will affect all the decisions you make in running your business. It will determine your marketing strategy, the choice of location, the pricing of your product, and so on.

Let us recap the discussion just carried out. The important process we are describing consists of two steps:

1. Identify your competitors (and, therefore, your customers).
2. Choose how to position your product in that market segment.

To achieve the second point, you need to find the right message to convey: what makes your product better than the competition? It doesn't need to be better overall, but it must be better at something. Find that something and build your message around it. Think of the example above. Will your message be along the lines of "fast and healthy" or "made right for you"? Note that we are choosing *what* to say, not *how* to say it. **Positioning your product ultimately means deciding which message you wish to attach to it** and how you want the product to be perceived in the mind of your customers. It will be the role of marketing (see the next chapter) to tell you, after a careful study of your audience, how to best convey that message.

Here is a real-world example of a product whose fate was turned around by a successful positioning in the minds of customers: the Milk Duds. These candies were first created in 1928 when Hoffman and Co. of Chicago tried to manufacture a perfectly round, chocolate-covered caramel candy. Since it was impossible to make the candies round, they ended up being called "duds." At one point, the Milk Duds were struggling to survive, unable to compete with other more successful chocolate bars. Many supermarkets wouldn't even keep Milk Duds on their shelves; they could be found almost exclusively in the stores of movie theaters. Then someone in the company finally cracked the mystery: since Milk Duds come in boxes of 15 individual slow-eating caramels, they last longer than other candies. This was the reason why they were still going strong as movie theater treats: moviegoers could enjoy their snack longer during the film than if they bought other chocolate bars. The team behind Milk Duds thus decided to try a new way to position their product for customers: *the long-lasting candy bar.*

The company's marketing team set to work on this idea and produced an ingenious commercial featuring a kid who at first is disappointed after devouring a chocolate bar in a few seconds. Later the same kid appears happy and satisfied while slowly chewing his Milk Duds. This new message of *a long-lasting treat* resonated far beyond movie theaters and eventually made Milk Duds one of the most successful candy products on the market. Note that the product was saved not by changing it but by finding a new position for it in the minds of candy buyers. To this day, we can read on the Amazon page of the Milk Duds, "the delicious taste of chocolate and chewy caramel will last all the way to the closing credits."

There is a lot to learn from the Milk Duds story, and it is not a lesson specific to the food industry. Whatever you are selling, be it a product or a service, and in whatever fashion, whether at a corner store or online, the path to follow is the same: after having determined your competitors and your target audience, you must **find your special position within the segment of the market you have identified.** Do as the people behind the Milk Duds and ask yourself what is different and unique about your product. Take your time to reflect carefully on these points. Effective positioning can make a fortune from a modest product, while misguided positioning can kill a great product.

Only after having carefully carried out the analysis described above can you decide the price of the product or service that you are offering. **A common mistake for businesses is to price their products too low**. There are three main reasons behind this error, and they are all connected to some false beliefs which deserve to be exposed and debunked.

False Belief #1: New products cannot compete with the market's giants. This idea is so pervasive that sometimes it is shared, even unconsciously, by the new entrepreneurs themselves, who, as a result, undervalue what they have to offer. Lacking confidence in their product, they end up setting too low a price, hoping in that way to attract customers.

False Belief #2: People generally buy the least expensive stuff. This is simply not true. If something is really useful or trendy, rest assured that people will find the money for it. Even people who struggle financially sometimes buy iPhones, AirPods, jewelry, expensive beauty products, and handbags. Do you have the feeling that nobody will buy your product or use your service unless it is priced at the lowest level? Maybe you don't want to say it out loud or even admit it to yourself, but you do share that thought to a certain extent. Get rid of it immediately. It is the result of widespread misconceptions. If there is real quality in your product, and marketing and positioning are done properly, price won't be an issue, and your business will be successful.

False Belief #3: It is easier to make money by selling at a low price. This is how the fallacy is usually spelled out: "Maybe I won't make a high profit on a single item, but with a lower price, I will sell more items, thus profiting from the high volume of sales." It sounds reasonable, doesn't it? Everyone knows that lower prices bring more customers. There is nothing wrong with that part of the argument. However, what most people tend to forget is that there are high costs embedded in dealing with a large number of clients. First of all, you need to hire more staff. If you have a physical location, you will have to restock more frequently, as well as pay much higher cleaning expenses. Even if you are selling a service online, you will need to hire people not to decrease the quality of your customer service. Should you start your business on a large scale in order to be able to absorb a high number of customers? In the previous chapter, we have already discussed compelling reasons why you shouldn't.

Think about the companies offering the lowest prices in the market. Who sells the cheapest groceries? Where do you find the cheapest coffee? Where are the cheapest burgers? Your answers will be based on your personal experience, but I bet that you will name three huge corporations. It's not surprising at all. Their massive size is the reason why they can afford such low prices. So, accept that, at the moment, it's impossible for you to make a profit selling $1 cheeseburgers. You can't compete with McDonald's, at least not yet. Or better, you must position your cheeseburgers differently.

I have made what I hope is a strong case for why very low prices are not recommended. How should you then price your product? Before answering, allow me to take you on a small detour.

Look around you and pick up the first pen you can find. An average BIC ballpoint pen at Walmart costs around 10 cents. Those are the pens I usually get, and you probably have just picked up something similar from your desk. When I want to treat myself, I sometimes buy a gel pen for a dollar or two. Once I received for my birthday a fancy pen with my initials engraved. A quick search online revealed that my uncle must have spent around $30 on it. That's about it, right? How much more can you even spend on a pen? Well, the most expensive in the world sells for $8.1 million. Yes, you have read correctly; it's $8.1 million. We are talking about *Fulgor Nocturnus*, a fountain pen crafted with rare black diamonds produced by the celebrated Italian pen maker Tibaldi.

The purpose of this little digression was to show you that even for an object as simple as a pen, the price range is extreme. Back to us. How will you price your product? Likely, you are producing neither the equivalent of a BIC nor something as deluxe as the Fulgor Nocturnus. Try to assess honestly and objectively where your product is placed within that wide range and set your price accordingly. In doing so, pay attention not to fall for the false beliefs described above. Make sure instead to:

1. Value your work.
2. Set a price that you find fair to compensate for your efforts.
3. Stay away from the bottom prices.

Don't forget to also ask yourself how much you are trying to make by selling your product. Remember that not all the sales revenue will end up in your pocket: there are taxes, operating expenses, and money that you will not want to take out of the business because they will serve as reinvestment. Set a price that is consistent with your earning goal.

In the end, your aim is to find an **efficient price**, that is, a price that is as close as possible to the maximum that customers are prepared to pay. When you are trying to give shape to your entrepreneurial ideas, consider your needs first. After all, prices are not engraved in stone, and you will always be able to go back and adjust them later.

8

Networking and Collaborations

Networking is the exchange of information and ideas among people with a common profession or special interest, usually in an informal social setting. There are several good reasons why networking is important for you:

- You can learn from the experience of other young entrepreneurs who might have overcome challenges similar to the ones you are facing at the moment.
- It gives you a chance to promote your business and get yourself noticed.
- It opens the door for new business opportunities and partnerships.
- You can benefit from the support, mentorship, and advice of high-profile individuals in your field.
- It gives a boost to your self-confidence.

Unfortunately, most of the networking happening these days is highly inefficient. It usually consists of a superficial conversation followed by an exchange of business cards that are destined to lie forgotten inside a wallet. You should avoid that kind of poor networking at all costs! So, what are the best strategies to make your networking efficient?

Networking Advice #1: Don't waste your time. Don't go to networking events indiscriminately, especially if they are in person, and you can't just excuse yourself and log off. Online there are many platforms that connect people who are starting the same type of business. There, users discuss common issues, share their experiences and success stories, and give each other feedback. Such interactions can be invaluable if managed in the right way. But be careful because they could also be a huge waste of time. Always remember: time is your most valuable resource at the beginning of an enterprise. Here is how not to waste it while networking. Write down explicitly what you want from people and what kind of advice you are looking for. Why do you want to connect with them? What questions are you going to ask? On which issue precisely are you in need of feedback? Be efficient and specific. Knowing exactly what you want will guide you. Once you have this complete list of questions in front of your eyes, you can start looking for people to connect with. Only engage with people who you think will be useful to you, those who will likely know the answers to the questions on your list. Make sure every person you talk to is really worth your time!

Networking Advice #2: Follow up with the right people. Let's say you have met a high-profile person in your field at a networking event. You have introduced yourself briefly, and then you exchanged business cards. What is going to happen then? If you are really interested in talking more in-depth with this person, make sure you follow up soon with an email. It shouldn't be a long email. Simply remind them of who you are, at which event you met, and what you talked about in your first encounter. Tell them what topic you would be interested in discussing further and suggest a specific time and date for a meeting, either online or in person. Offering a specific date and time will make things concrete. Even if that doesn't work for them, they will be more likely to suggest an alternative.

Networking Advice #3: Offer something in return. Let's say you want important advice from someone or maybe even wish for their mentorship. Are you just going to show up to them and say, "Hey, can you be my mentor?".

Why should they do that for you? Why should they take time from their busy schedule for your sole benefit? You must approach them differently and, above all, offer something in return. You need to show them that there is value in you and they are not just giving away their time. For instance, you could say, "I have noticed the following weaknesses in your social media presence. Here are three things I would improve". Offer value based on your strength. If you have started networking, you must have identified your strengths by now. Show them to the people you want to connect with and use them as leverage to get what you want. At some point in your business, you might want to or even have to hire collaborators. What are the characteristics you should look for in the people you employ? Here are the three traits that identify your perfect collaborator:

- **Skilled.** The most successful chiefs are those who are not afraid to hire people who are better than them.
- **Hard-working.** Of course, any skill is useless if it isn't backed up by energy and a drive to put it to use.
- **Honest.** Don't neglect this point. You want to be able to fully trust the people who work alongside you. They should care about the success of your business as if it was their own.

9

Choosing an Online Business

While nowadays we often take the Internet for granted, we should constantly marvel at its immense power and at the endless possibilities it offers. Are you passionate about windsurfing, bee harvesting, or 3D chess? There are more than seven billion humans on this planet, and therefore, no matter how specific and peculiar your interests are, without a doubt, they are shared by at least a few tens of thousands of people. By going online, you can find windsurfers, bee harvesters, and 3D chess players from all over the world in a very short time and from the comfort of your home. With a few clicks, you can connect with those people, exchange information, and even conduct business. How mind-blowing is that? Only a few decades ago, it would have been considered science fiction.

Did you know that there is a community of people who send their toys on trips? They often create a social media profile for each itinerant toy, complete with a wish list of activities that the toy "would like to do" during the visit. Hosts and owners then keep the toy's profile updated with pictures and videos from the trip. Are we digressing? Yes and no. Remember that every niche provides new and exciting business opportunities. Whenever you identify something that people care about, you have found a market.

Imagine you were born in a Welsh coal-mining town in the early 1900s.

Certainly, you don't have much choice in how to live your life. Let's assume you are a boy. At age thirteen, you have to start your back-breaking work down the pit, which you will continue until you are too old or too weak to be useful. Not many alternative careers are available, if any at all. Why is there only one occupation for you? Because mining coal is the only way in which you, as a healthy young man, can produce value within that community. In case you want to do something else, you have to leave your family and move elsewhere (if that is an option). This has been a common situation throughout most of human history.

The Internet has changed the game completely, creating many new ways to produce value for yourself and for what is nowadays a unique global community. If you have a laptop and Internet access, your possibilities to make money are virtually infinite, regardless of where you live or what the people around you are doing. Among the countless online activities in which you can engage, you can even pick the one that best resonates with your interests because no matter how uncommon these are, the web gives you the opportunity to find your audience.

It all sounds amazing, but how can you put these thoughts into practice when you want to start your own online business? What should you do?

First of all, here is what you shouldn't do: **don't just copy others**.

I know Bob is making money online with that activity, but I think I'll give it a try myself. This attitude is as common as it is misguided. Maybe you will make a few bucks that way, but if you are reading this book, it is because you are ambitious. You don't want to simply scrap by. You are striving for success, and to be successful, you need to engage in something that is truly yours, something that lights the fire of passion inside you. Only that way will you be able to keep your focus, express your full potential, and profit in the long term.

Keep this in mind: in online business, there isn't a clear separation between activities that are profitable and others that are not. **Whether a specific enterprise makes money or not depends entirely on you.**

For instance, there are people who earn money online by doing the following:

- Dubbing over famous movies or cartoons with funny accents.
- Discussing macabre stories and gruesome crime news.
- Vlogging from supermarkets in foreign countries, commenting on what can be found on the shelves.

These are people who are talented at making hilarious voices, have a morbid interest in death, or love traveling and are curious about the habits of foreign countries. They were able to create a profitable business out of their interests and skills. Great! Does it mean that if you start doing one of the three things above, you will also make money? Absolutely not. Doing exactly what other people are doing will lead you nowhere. You can and should be inspired by the experiences and success stories of others, but you must also be original and walk your own separate way. **You need to provide some added value in order to conquer your share of the market.**

You can't be a better version of someone else, but you can be the best version of yourself. Let me say it once more. Virtually anything can be made profitable nowadays on the Internet; its success depends only on you.

Therefore, in choosing an online business to pursue, there is no point in asking, "What works? What is most profitable?" You should instead ask, "What will work **for me**?" Make yourself the starting point of your search. As a first step, make sure you truly understand who you are.

Here are the three most important aspects you should consider when choosing which online business to undertake.

Aspect #1: Your passions. What do you like to do? And I don't mean simply as a hobby or an activity to which you want to dedicate a few hours over the weekend. Think of something that you genuinely like. What is the stuff that you can talk about for hours? It could be literally anything, even related to pastimes you have always considered futile, like watching TV shows or reading comic books. Remember, where there is interest, there is a market and, therefore, business opportunities.

We have already seen how there is a stigma, especially among working-class families, surrounding online enterprises which are not seen as legitimate businesses. You will have to fight against this prejudice. Do not talk to anyone while you are trying to assess your true interests. Your friends and family members might also share that preconception, in which case they will try to redirect your ambitions toward a more traditional brick-and-mortar face-to-face business. Don't let anyone tell you what you like and what you don't. You are the only one who is entitled to express an opinion on this point.

Here are some data that you should find encouraging if what you came up with is along the lines of TV shows and comics. According to the Bureau of Labor Statistics, the average American household spent over $3,000 on entertainment in 2019. That amount is far greater than what was spent on apparel ($1,883) or education ($1,443).

Aspect #2: Your strengths. What are you good at? Where do your talents lie? This is a crucial point because you need to be realistic when assessing the prospects of your enterprise. Let's say you have identified baseball as your primary passion. If, despite your drive and motivation, you are not that great of a player, you will not count on a professional career in the MLB, but you can still look for some business opportunities related to your favorite sport. You could start a baseball podcast, sell merchandise, or manage an online community of fans.

When assessing your strengths, it is also important to ask other people. You might think you are great at stand-up comedy, but if nobody laughs at your routine, then maybe you should reconsider. At the end of the day, it is the judgment of other people that will decree the success of your enterprise. Your products and services need to be appreciated by your customers, and nobody will compensate you for what you think you are good at. So, ask the people closest to you what, in their opinion, are your best talents. Then compare their lists to the one you made yourself.

Aspect #3: **Your personality**. Are you an introvert or an extrovert? Do you want more or less contact with customers? Do you feel comfortable in a technical job where you work behind the scenes? Or do you see yourself more in a public-oriented position, building an online community and engaging with your audience?

Consider each of these questions carefully and keep your answers into account when deciding which activity within the niche that interests you is the best fit for you. The message of this chapter can be condensed into a single sentence: **build your business around you, starting from your passions, talents, and personality traits.**

It is a clear and simple principle on which you should never compromise. Do not try to be what you are, not just pursue a venture that you think is profitable. Stay true to yourself! Being a successful entrepreneur ultimately means bringing out your true self and realizing your full potential.

10

Conclusions: Ten Rules for New Entrepreneurs

Starting your own business is not easy. Growing it into a prosperous and rewarding activity is even more difficult. However, once you get all the wrinkles ironed out, the benefits of owning your business are countless. Not to mention the fact that the challenges you must overcome will make you a better person overall, improving your life and your personal relationships.

Every success story is different and individual, and therefore there is no royal road to success. But there are certainly some guiding principles that can help you find your way and accomplish your professional goals. I have tried to collect in this book the most important ones. In this last chapter, I want to summarize the message of the book in ten rules. Write them down on a piece of paper and look at them periodically to check if you are still following these fundamental rules.

Rule #1: **Cultivate the right mindset**. Convince yourself that you have a right to be happy and wealthy and that it is possible to attain your goals. Get rid of all the negative core beliefs that are holding you back and reprogram your mind for success using the techniques described in the first part of this book.

Rule #2: **Keep learning**. Be open-minded and curious, always willing to learn new things. Remember that the average CEO of a big corporation reads one book a week. You may be talented, smart, and creative, but running a business is a complex activity that involves many different skills. Be prepared to face everyday new and different challenges every day.

Rule #3: **Learn about cash flow, capital, and credit**. Review what you have learned in the chapter of this book dedicated to this topic and take that as the starting point of your research. Do some more reading online and buy valuable courses or books on that subject. It won't be wasted money if you are investing in your financial education.

Rule #4: **Build your product around you**. Don't jump onto some opportunity just because you think it will make money. Consider your personality, your strengths, and your desires. Those should be the starting point for deciding what product or service you are going to offer to your audience.

Rule #5: **Start small**. Every big corporation had humble beginnings. Don't worry about the lack of startup capital, and don't compare yourself to big corporations. Being small has its advantages, namely, being better and faster at changing and customizing your offer. Exploit those advantages to optimize your product or service. Make it original and valuable for your target audience. Your goal at the beginning is to find your niche and dominate it. Walk your own path and try not to feel the pressure of the competition of big businesses. Be sure of your value. Even if you are initially successful, don't be in a hurry to scale up. Expanding a business too rapidly can have a negative impact on your finances. Don't make the mistake of opening multiple locations or paying for too much advertising. Remember that in the initial stage, being everywhere is being nowhere.

Rule #6: Don't neglect marketing. A common mistake of new entrepreneurs is to think that their business will automatically be supported by their friends, family, or their local community. Don't run on this assumption. Don't take anything for granted. Success always comes from delivering the right product to the right audience, and marketing is fundamental to reaching that audience. Do your market research not only when you are ready to sell but also before and during the development of your product.

Rule #7: Don't undersell your product. Give up the idea that you need to keep humble, that having success is somehow undeserved, unjust, or shameful. On the contrary, success requires no apologies. Trying to appease the community by charging low prices won't work. It will make you fail, thus depriving everyone of what you can offer. So, stop the feeling that charging more than the bare minimum is unjust, and be realistic. Give value to your work and try to reach the right customers, that is, those that are able and willing to pay the price that your product is worth.

Rule #8: Pursue efficient networking. Follow the networking advice contained in this book. Exchanging ideas with your peers is fundamental to the growth of your enterprise.

Rule #9: Don't upgrade your lifestyle too soon. Not all the revenue from your business will end up in your pocket. Every enterprise has its running costs, and you must always keep that in mind. Don't buy an expensive car as soon as you come across enough money to do so. Owning a business brings with it certain responsibilities. There will probably be times of scarcity, and therefore you must start saving immediately to ensure the long-term survival of your activity.

Rule #10: Learn from your mistakes. It is normal and even healthy to make mistakes. As we have already said, the only people who don't make mistakes are those who do not even try. However, you should try to keep them small and, at the same time, learn from them. Don't let a failure bring you down but see it instead as an opportunity for growing and improving.

More than half of the people in their twenties in the United States hope to become entrepreneurs at some point in the future. Hope is not enough. That is why so few manage to realize that wish. You want to be different; you want to be part of the successful minority. To achieve that, you must stop hoping and start acting. This book gives you the right tools to begin your journey on a proven path to success.

III

Book 3: Setting Up Your Business

11

What is an LLC?

An LLC (Limited Liability Company) is the most popular type of business structure. The first US-based LLC was created in Wyoming in 1977. By the year 1996, LLC statutes had been established in all 50 states. The basic idea was to allow business owners to create a tax-friendly company while maintaining a level of protection for their personal assets.

Because of its flexibility and simplicity, the popularity of the LLC business structure has grown exponentially. Today, there are over 21 million LLCs in the United States compared to approximately 1.7 million traditional C-Corporations.

Let's assume that you are a small business owner or an entrepreneur. Then you have several choices to give a legal structure to your activity: sole proprietorships, general partnerships, corporations, LLCs, etc. The structure you choose for your business will determine who owns the business, how taxes are paid, and who is liable in case of a lawsuit or debts. In most cases, starting an LLC is the simplest and most effective way to protect your assets, establish credibility, and save on your taxes.

Let us consider some of the main reasons why it may be worth opening an LLC.

An **LLC is its own legal entity**, separate from its owners. This creates what is known as a 'corporate veil' between you as a person and the activities of your business. Having an LLC keeps the owner's personal assets secure in the event of a lawsuit or unpaid business debt.

Being a legal entity means that the LLC as a corporation has its own legal responsibilities (which include tax filing) as well as legal rights. For instance, it can enter into contracts either as a vendor or a supplier and can sue or be sued in a court of law.

LLCs have pass-through taxation. That is, you are not taxed at the entity level. When a corporation makes a profit, that profit is taxed, distributed to the owners, and then taxed again as personal income. **An LLC's profits are not taxed**. The income passes straight to the business owner, who only pays personal income taxes for their share of the business.

For LLCs, there are no strict requirements for record keeping. Business accounting and compliance can be complicated and confusing, especially for a beginner entrepreneur. LLCs, compared to other corporate structures, simplify the formation and keeping of business records, making them easy to maintain even for single-owner businesses.

In summary, an LLC allows you to protect your assets, pay fewer taxes and reduce paperwork. But that is not all. There are many other reasons why you might want to start your LLC, including privacy or the fact that owners of an LLC need not be US citizens or permanent residents. We will look more in-depth at the advantages and possibilities offered by LLCs later in the book. But first, let's take a look at the different types of LLCs.

12

Different Types of LLCs

As if choosing a business structure was not enough, you also have to choose among different types of LLCs. But don't worry. If you have a clear goal in mind, it will be easy to pick the type of LLC that is most suitable for your business.

Single-Member LLC (SMLLC)

The name is self-explanatory. A single-member limited liability company has only one owner or member. That individual bears the full responsibility of the company, including being accountable for tax payments.

This is by far the most popular form of LLC used by beginner entrepreneurs or freelancers. They start out with a single-member LLC and still enjoy the freedom of adding partners to their business at a later time.

Having the option of incorporating more partners can be essential when raising funds and trying to grow your company. At that stage, you might want to transition to a Multi-Member LLC.

Multi-Member LLC (MMLLC)

Once again, the name is self-explanatory. An MMLLC has multiple owners. These can be individuals, other LLCs, or corporations. Although technically, an MMLC can have an arbitrary number of members, the most popular type is a two-member LLC for businesses run by a husband/wife couple or by two friends who act as partners.

The most important difference between an SMLLC and an MMLLC concerns the way in which taxes are paid.

The IRS treats an SMLLC as a "disregarded entity." That is, **the income generated by the LLC is reported on the owner's personal federal tax return**. In other words, no separate federal tax return is necessary for the SMLLC. This process is called "pass-through taxation." The sole owner of the LLC is personally responsible for paying the taxes for the income generated by the business.

Multi-member LLCs, instead, are treated by the IRS as partnerships. **A multiple-member LLC must file a tax return** and give its members K-1 forms to file with their returns. Unsurprisingly, having more members means more paperwork.

There is another aspect in which a single-member LLC differs from a multi-member one. While it is highly recommended to have an operating agreement in both cases, as we will see more in detail later, in the case of a multiple-member company, the drafting of this document requires a much higher degree of attention. You must make sure that the rights of each member are clearly spelled out, especially in the case of events that will break the partnership, such as the death of one of the members or an irreconcilable disagreement. Prevention is better than cure.

SMLLC or MMLLC?

It seems like an easy choice, and most of the time, it is. If you are alone in your business, then you should probably go for an SMLLC, while if you have one or more business partners, then your best option is likely an MMLC. However, you should keep an open mind and **consider the advantages and disadvantages of both options.**

There are cases in which it is convenient for a single business owner to form a multiple-member company. For instance, they might want to add their spouse or parents as members to gain further asset protection. On the other hand, there are situations in which it is convenient for two or more people in a partnership to start single-member companies. This often happens in real estate investing.

Consider the following example. Alice and Bob are in a 50% partnership and bought ten properties as separate LLCs. To simplify their taxes, they made all these SMLLCs owned by an MMLLC, of which they are both members. With this strategy, they avoid having to file a separate tax return for each property. Remember that **a single-member LLC is easier to manage for tax purposes because, as a "disregarded entity," no federal tax return is required.**

The example in the previous paragraph introduces us to another important distinction, which is the one between holding LLCs and operating LLCs.

Holding LLC

A **holding LLC** is a company that exists only to hold assets, like real estate, or to act as an umbrella holding company for other subsidiary companies. In the example of Alice and Bob, they have ten operating LLCs and one holding LLC.

Holding companies are created to have additional layers of protection and, in some cases, as in the example above, to simplify taxes. Your first LLC will surely be an operating company, but as your business grows, keep in mind the option of instituting this further level of protection from liability.

Member-Managed LLC vs. Manager-Managed LLC

A Member-Managed LLC is one where one of the owners runs the daily operations of the company. This is the usual structure and the one that most likely applies to you. The other option is a Manager-Managed LLC, where the operations of the company are run by someone different than the owners. This model mostly applies to LLCs started by investors who prefer not to be involved in the day-to-day running of the company.

Domestic LLC vs. Foreign LLC

What is a Foreign LLC? Despite the name, it doesn't mean that the company comes from another country. Instead, it means your business was organized under the laws of a different state. **An LLC is domestic in the state where it is created and foreign everywhere else.**

When you conduct business outside of the state in which the LLC was created, you are required to register your company as a Foreign LLC (you must obtain the so-called "foreign qualification"). Registration is used to make sure that your company meets the regulations and tax requirements of the foreign state.

A company needs to acquire foreign qualifications when it grows and expands its business into other states. But it is also common for LLCs to be formed in states with business-friendly tax laws and operate as foreign companies in their home state.

One or many LLCs?

As we will see in the next chapters, opening and maintaining an LLC has certain costs. If you are involved in several businesses, you might be wondering whether it is worth opening a new LLC for each of your projects. The answer is not so straightforward and depends on your individual situation.

There are definitely benefits to keeping all your activities under the same LLC. For instance, taxes are easier to manage, and the costs of maintenance of the company can be shared by the different businesses. The biggest con is that any project is liable for the losses and debts of the others. You can't just file bankruptcy for the business that has failed and let it go under. Instead, your successful projects will have to pay off the debts of this failed business.

It is recommended to keep all your activities under the same LLC if the following circumstances apply:

- You have the same ownership structure in all your businesses. For instance, if all are solo projects.
- Your projects are relatively low risk, so you are not taking on debt.
- You are not likely to get sued, and therefore you are not worried about the liabilities issues of the projects to each other.
- Many of your projects are experimental, that is, new ideas that you are just testing out. In this case, it is better to keep the business structure lean and simple by operating all your activities under the same LLC.

You should create a different LLC for each business if you find yourself in the following circumstances.

- The ownership structure is different for each business. For instance, one project is solo, and another is in partnership.
- One (or more) of the businesses is high risk. If one project is taking a lot

of debt, has lots of employees, or might be involved in litigation, then it is appropriate to keep it separate from your other businesses.

· If you are developing a branch of your business with the purpose of selling it, then it would be better to have it under a separate entity.

In any case, it is always wise to investigate possible tax benefits coming from separating your business activities into different LLCs.

13

Advantages and Disadvantages of an LLC

What are the Advantages of an LLC?

Business owners have plenty of advantages when they register their business as an LLC:

- **You only have limited liability.** As an owner, you are not personally responsible for the debts or liabilities of the business. When an LLC is set up properly, the assets of the owners are not used to pay off business debts. LLC assets, on the other hand, are used to wipe out debts.
- **Pass-through taxation.** Usually, the LLC is not taxed at the business level. The owner reports the income or loss of the LLC on his/her personal federal tax return. Therefore, it is the business owner who pays any due taxes.
- **Flexible distribution of losses and profits among owners.** Owners have flexibility in distributing losses and profits among the owners of the LLC.
- **No restrictions regarding the ownership of the LLC.** An LLC does not have a limit of fifty owners as an S corporation does. At most, there are very few ownership restrictions, but typically there are none.
- **No strictness regarding management.** LLC owners have a free hand in

structuring the management of the company.

- **Various classes of membership.** Unlike in S corporations, where there is only one class of membership, for LLCs, there are various membership classes available. These are established in the Operating Agreement of the company.
- **Less bureaucracy.** LLCs have less yearly paperwork than C corporations and S corporations. They also do not have to comply with meeting requirements imposed on C and S corporations.
- **Trustworthiness.** Registering your company as an LLC may help increase the trustworthiness of your business. Typically an LLC is perceived as more legitimate than a business registered as a general partnership or a sole proprietorship.
- **Consent in written form is required to add new owners or increase the ownership of an LLC.** The consent must be provided before ownership is given to others.

What Are the Disadvantages of an LLC?

It is not completely risk-free. Although an LLC is responsible and assumes all the risk if the company is sued, you still risk losing your business. For instance, if you run an interior design company and damage your client's property or injure your client, she can sue your company. If she wins a large amount of damages, she might be able to take all of your tools and money.

It costs more to set up. Registering a company as an LLC requires more legal paperwork, and you incur more costs than if you choose to register it as a sole proprietorship. Some of these costs include expenses for the paperwork you need to file with the state and the formation fee. Typically you can get a free business Employer Identification Number (EID), but you still have to fill out the paperwork and apply.

An LLC might not be worthwhile for your business. In certain cases, businesses do not earn enough or might not make enough profits for the tax benefits of operating an LLC to outweigh the costs.

You pay taxes on all profits. An LLC is a pass-through entity. That is, you personally get the profits and pay taxes on your business at your personal tax rate. You benefit because the personal tax rate is lower than the C or S corporation tax rate. However, you are taxed on all of your profits, i.e., even if you want to keep money in your business for further investments in your company. Said otherwise, you will be unable to make tax-deductible investments in your business. (There are some exceptions related to the set-up costs of your LLC). It is recommended to hire a tax advisor to find out whether an LLC makes sense for you in this case.

Profits are subject to Social Security taxes. In certain cases, the owners of an LLC could end up paying more in taxes than those of a corporation since both salaries and profits are subject to self-employment taxes. They currently amount to 15.3% – 12.4% for Social Security and 2.9% for Medicare. When a company is registered as a corporation, only salaries are subject to taxation.

Profits must be recognized straight away. LLCs are not subject to double taxation. This means that the profits generated by an LLC are reported automatically in the members' income. In contrast, C-corporations do not have to distribute profits to shareholders straight away. Therefore, shareholders do not always have to pay taxes on the profits of the corporation.

Fringe benefits and taxable income. The fringe benefits received by the employees of an LLC, such as medical insurance or parking, must be treated as taxable income. In contrast, C-corporation employees who also receive fringe benefits do not have to pay income taxes on the benefits they receive.

14

Is an LLC Right for You?

Choosing your business structure can be one of the most intimidating steps of your business. You have already found a market, you have an idea, and your clients are ready to pay for your product or service. You now find yourself researching the different business structures and wondering which one is the best choice for your business. Is it better to keep it simple and be a sole proprietor, or should you have a corporation? Should you choose the middle ground and opt for an LLC instead?

Many different structures exist to meet the needs of various types of businesses. For instance, an S-Corporation has a board of directors and shareholders. They must hold annual meetings and record minutes. An LLC, on the other hand, does not have the same formal requirements. This is one of the reasons why an LLC is a good fit for many small to medium-sized businesses. It allows business owners to form a legitimate business (with liability protections) without many of the formal requirements necessary for a corporation.

When deciding whether to form an LLC or some other entity, business owners look at the benefits and risks of each structure and weigh them against the needs of their business. Next, they choose the structure that best fits their business needs.

Here are some questions you should ask yourself to decide if an LLC is the right choice for you:

Am I working by myself or with others?

Regardless if you start a business with your best friend from childhood or with an acquaintance you met at a dinner, partnering with someone entails a lot of risks. The effort it takes to register your business as an LLC pales in comparison to the potential negative consequences you may have to face if your partnership goes downhill. When you opt for an LLC, you ensure that the LLC - not you - will be liable in case your business partner makes a bad decision.

Will I be at risk of getting sued?

Did you know that between 36% and 53% of all small businesses get sued every year and that a whopping 43% are threatened with lawsuits? Moreover, 90% of all businesses are sued at least one time during their lifespan. As you can see from these numbers, business owners are far more likely than private persons to be sued, and this is not surprising at all. There are certain risks that come with providing a service or selling a product. Your clients might be dissatisfied with the product, delayed delivery might have negative repercussions, and unexpected events might displease some of your customers in an irreconcilable way. Therefore, it is almost always better to form an LLC not to put your personal assets at risk.

If the risk of being sued is particularly high for your business, an LLC is the recommended choice. Here is how you can determine if you have a high-risk business:

- You have employees who are at risk of injuring themselves during

working hours.
- Customers may suffer harm when using your product (e.g., cosmetic products).
- Your customers could claim that you provided a service that was below the professional standard of care (e.g., medical malpractice).
- You work with suppliers or consumers who might sue you for breaching a contract.
- Your employees could file a lawsuit for discrimination or unjustified termination.

Note: Some states will not allow you to form an LLC if you are a licensed professional. Therefore, you might want to consider forming a corporation or a professional limited liability company instead.

Is this a side gig?

Is this a small, low-risk business that you work on besides your job? Is your goal just to make a little money on the side? Then an LLC might not be the most suitable structure for you. The amount of effort it takes to form an LLC is just not worth it for such a small business, especially if the LLC fees in your state are so high that they significantly diminish your profit.

What are my future plans for my business?

One of the factors that you should take into consideration when choosing your business structure is the future of your company. An LLC reduces the liability of the owner and offers protection similar to a corporation. Nevertheless, there are certain cases in which you might need a corporation instead of an LLC. For instance, the owners of a corporation own shares of stocks in their business. On the other hand, LLC owners own equity in the assets of their business. If you plan to sell shares of stocks in your business in the future, the prerequisite is that your business is registered as a corporation. Therefore, it is important to consider how you envision the future of your business when deciding whether to create an LLC.

15

Should You Create an LLC Holding Company?

What Is a Holding Company?

A holding company, or umbrella company, is a parent business entity, that is, a corporation with subsidiaries. These subsidiaries are separate businesses that are wholly or partially owned by the parent. The holding company itself does not conduct any standard business operations, which are left to the subsidiaries. Specifically, the holding company does not manufacture any products, nor does it sell any products or services. As the name suggests, the holding company only holds stocks or other forms of ownership in the child companies (subsidiaries).

While a holding company does not conduct business operations on its own, it owns other companies that may sell services and products or manufacture goods. It may also hold other assets such as real estate properties or real estate portfolios, vehicles, equipment, or anything else that can be of value to the operations of the subsidiaries of the holding company. One of the most famous holding companies is Warren Buffett's Berkshire Hathaway. The company owns and controls many different businesses, such as GEICO and Dairy Queen.

A holding company may own 100% of a subsidiary, or it can simply have enough interest to maintain control through voting rights. This usually means any share of ownership that is above 51%. Having this sort of control gives the holding company the power to run and oversee the activities of the child companies. For instance, the management team of an LLC holding company can elect or remove directors or managers. They can also make major policy decisions, such as merging or even dissolving a subsidiary. However, each child company has its own management who runs the day-to-day operations. The management of each child company can make decisions about internal operations such as hiring, firing, and how to operate more effectively and efficiently. The people running the holding company do not participate in the managing of the business operations of their subsidiaries.

How Can an LLC Holding Company Be Financed?

The people who run the holding company are responsible for deciding where to invest its money. They have to constantly ask themselves questions such as "Should we buy more real estate?", "Should we buy a manufacturing plant?" or "What other assets would be valuable to our holding company?".

Holding companies usually have three different ways to raise money:

1. **Selling equity** or interest in the holding company. This means that the company will be recruiting other people interested in having stocks in the holding company or in any of its subsidiaries.
2. **Borrowing money** from other investors or banks.
3. **Reinvesting its profits** from the subsidiaries, such as dividends, distributions, or rent payments. Raising money as an LLC holding company tends to be easier than for an operating LLC because there are more members involved, and the company itself owns more assets.

How Can a Holding Company Be Used?

A holding company can be used by any type of business regardless of size or industry. Therefore, **small businesses or even single-member entrepreneurs can start a holding company.**

Let us consider the following example. Imagine that you want to buy an apartment as a real estate investment. You should consider the option of forming two LLCs. One LLC would own the apartment building, and the other LLC would be the holding company. If later on you want to expand your investment, you can raise money by selling shares in your existing holding company. With the money raised, you might, for instance, buy a profitable e-commerce company that is already set up as an LLC. After making this acquisition, you would still have one holding company with a new partner. Together, you would own two businesses. One would be the apartment building investment, and the other the e-commerce store.

Here comes the interesting part. When you have a holding company with multiple assets that drive revenue and profitability, then you can position your holding company for a major buyout. You could sell your holding company for millions of dollars to large investment firms or venture capitalists who are keen on closing big deals. In fact, many publicly traded companies on the stock market are holding companies that constantly try to improve their revenues and increase the price per share of their stocks. Interestingly enough, many people who buy stocks don't even realize that they are investing in a holding company and not the actual operating company.

The main point to keep in mind is that holding companies are more ubiquitous than one might think. Small holding companies have a greater chance (than operating companies) of being acquired by larger holding companies.

Advantages of an Umbrella Company

Liability protection. By having a parent LLC (the holding company) and multiple child LLCs (the subsidiaries), you have complete separation of each entity. This provides powerful liability protection between each entity because the debts of each subsidiary belong solely to that subsidiary. If we go back to the e-commerce example, imagine that your e-commerce store is struggling, and you are not able to pay off some of its debt. In that case, the creditor cannot go after the apartment building owned by the holding company. Creditors are only entitled to the assets that belong to the e-commerce store. Please note that it is important to be careful about the documents you sign. If you sign an agreement saying that you are personally liable for any debts or obligations, then your LLC cannot protect you against that.

Strong financing ability. Having an LLC holding company makes it easier for you to raise money. As mentioned before, you can raise money from other members of your holding company by selling interest in your companies or by seeking outside investment opportunities. Typically, a start-up or a new business is considered to be a great credit risk and may struggle with getting any type of investment. In contrast, when you have an established holding company, the investment is perceived as less risky. And it is not just a perception. If you obtain a loan with your holding company and then divert it to a start-up subsidiary, it is not only the start-up that is on the hook for that loan but the entire parent company.

Lower management needs. Each holding company will have its own management team to run the day-to-day operations. The holding company members simply make strategic investment decisions. These types of decisions don't require as much time as managing a company's daily activities, thus giving the owners a lot more flexibility.

A holding company may foster innovation. When you have a business that is doing extremely well as an entrepreneur, you try to do your best to maintain that positive momentum. Investing in a new idea or a start-up within that business can be risky and bring the momentum down. In contrast, when you have a holding company, you can simply place your new business idea or your new start-up idea into its own separate entity without compromising the other. (Check out also the section titled *One or many LLCs?*) For instance, in 2015, Google restructured and formed the holding company Alphabet (of which Google became a subsidiary) because they wanted to invest in other ventures, such as Google Glasses or Youtube, without compromising their core business.

Disadvantages of an Umbrella Company

Costs. The more entities you have, the higher your set-up costs and annual fees. It can cost anywhere between USD 100 to USD 500 per year per each LLC that you own. Besides that, each entity would also need its own books, so you have separate bookkeeping expenses. For this, as well as to keep track of taxes, you would need to hire someone part-time or full-time, which means additional costs. Costs are usually the main factor deterring people from starting holding companies.

Management challenges. Remember that a holding company is not involved in the day-to-day operations, but they do help elect the directors and managers of a subsidiary. Can you see the issue with this? Imagine the following scenario. You know ten times more than what your boss knows about the running of your business, yet she or he is the one to elect the managers of your company. If the wrong people are running the holding company, then they can drive the subsidiaries into failure.

Complexity. Holding companies often have more compliance requirements and are governed by local, state, and federal laws. Even the way your taxes are done will be completely different when you have a holding company. Therefore, you also need to maintain important documents, records, assets, liabilities, and other properties completely separate from one another. This requires a skill of extreme organization. If you end up mixing any of your assets, books, or financials together, then any creditor that is after you may also go after your other business assets due to the lack of separation. In conclusion, there are some great advantages of having a holding company, but if you aren't organized, or you don't hire help, you can find yourself with a huge headache trying to get everything sorted out.

To sum it up, just remember that an LLC holding company is a business entity that does not conduct business operations. Instead, it owns and controls other companies. Holding companies can help you grow your business and mitigate risks, but they can also be costly and complicated to manage.

16

How to Form an LLC?

How do you form an LLC?

A great option for small businesses and single-owners, LLCs are formal business structures recognized at the state and federal level that constitute a flexible and simple alternative to corporations. As we have already discussed, LLCs allow business owners to protect their personal assets, gain credibility, minimize taxes and streamline their administrative responsibilities.

Best of all, **they are easy and inexpensive to start**. There are two ways to start an LLC: You can form one yourself, or you can hire a service to do it for you. In this chapter, we will take a look at both options and help you decide how to go about forming your own Limited Liability Company.

Let's start by looking at how to form an LLC on your own, which requires a bit of work but can save you some money. The process does not require lots of complicated paperwork, and you can easily find all of the necessary forms online. Every state has different laws, and we recommend that you make yourself familiar with them depending on your preferred state.

Generally speaking, there are six steps you must take to start a new LLC.

Step One: Choose Your State

For most new business owners, the obvious option is to form an LLC in the state where you live and where you plan to conduct your business. When an LLC is first formed in a state, it is also known as a "Domestic LLC" in that state. If your business then expands to other states, your domestic LLC will need to be registered as a foreign LLC in every other state where you have a physical presence or employees. There are sometimes benefits to forming your LLC in a state with business-friendly laws, such as Delaware or Nevada. However, the tax advantages must be balanced against the extra fees and paperwork of having to register your LLC in multiple states.

Step Two: Choose a Name

Next, you will need to choose a name for your business. Every state has its own rules about what kind of names are allowed for LLCs. In general, you will need to observe these naming guidelines: Your name must include the phrase "limited liability company" or one of its abbreviations (LLC or L.L.C.). Restricted words such as Bank, Attorney, Law Office, etc., may require additional paperwork and may also need a licensed professional to be part of the LLC.

Your name cannot include words that could confuse your LLC with a government agency such as the FBI, Treasury, State Department, etc. You cannot use a name that has already been registered. To see if a name is available in your chosen state, you will need to perform a name search. You can do this for free on your state's Secretary of State website. We also recommend that you check to see if your business name is available as a web domain. Even if you don't plan to make a business website today, you may want to buy that URL in order to prevent others from acquiring it.

Step Three: Nominate a Registered Agent

At this point, you will need to nominate a registered agent for your LLC. Depending on your state, a registered agent is sometimes referred to as a resident agent, statutory agent, or agent for service of process. A registered agent is a person or business that acts as a point of contact for matters regarding your company. In fact, they send and receive legal papers on your behalf. Legal papers include any sort of official correspondence from legal summons to document filings. Your agent will receive these documents and then forward them to you. Your registered agent must be a resident of the state you're doing business in or a corporation authorized to conduct business in that state. If you nominate an individual, they can be a member of your LLC, including yourself. Most people, however, opt for using a registered agent company. Let's see why.

Technically, any person over 18 years old can be a registered agent, but there are some requirements that must be met:

- They must have a physical address (not just a post office box) in the state where your LLC is registered.
- They must be available in person during business hours at that address.

There might be some downsides to acting as your own registered agent. The first is privacy. Remember that the name and address of your registered agent are part of the public record. Therefore, if you are running your business from your house, you might not want to act as your own agent. Consider also that every time you move, you will have to promptly notify the state of your address change. Finally, remember that you must designate a registered agent in every state in which your company operates.

Step Four: File Formation Documents

To officially create an LLC, you will need to file formation documents with the secretary of state. The most common name for this document is "Articles of Organization." It is also known in some states as a "Certificate of Formation" or "Certificate of Organization." Your LLC formation document outlines the organizational structure of your business. The Articles of Organization require three primary pieces of information:

One: Your LLC's unique and legal name.

Two: The name and street address of your registered agent.

Three: You must decide who will act as the manager of the LLC.

There are two options: The first is Member-managed, where all members of the LLC manage the company. This is good for small organizations, where everyone is involved in day-to-day operations. The second option is manager-managed, where individuals other than the owners are appointed to manage the LLC. This second model is appropriate for larger organizations, where not everyone is involved in the day-to-day affairs of the business.

At this stage, you will also have to pay a one-time processing fee to the secretary of state. This cost varies per state, but the price ranges between 40 and 500 dollars, with an average of about 125 dollars. Once you have filed your Articles of Organization and paid the fees, the state will then process your application. Most states process an application in three to seven working days. If the application is successful, you will have officially formed an LLC. The most common reason why an application is rejected is that the LLC naming guidelines were not followed.

Step Five: Create an Operating Agreement

Although not every state requires it, you should always create an operating agreement to establish ownership terms and member roles for your LLC. This foundational document is the core of your LLC and will help you maintain your organization, as well as further establish your LLC as a separate legal entity. There are six main sections of an operating agreement:

- **Organization.** This section outlines when and where the company was created, who the members are, and how ownership is structured.
- **Management and Voting.** This section addresses how the company is managed, as well as how the members vote.
- **Capital Contributions.** This part concerns the financial aspects of the company. It should contain information such as which members financially support the LLC and in which ways the company will raise further funds in the future.
- **Distributions.** This section must cover how the company's profits and losses will be shared among members.
- **Membership Changes.** This section describes the process for adding or removing members. Moreover, it details when and how members can transfer their ownership shares.
- **Dissolution.** This section explains the circumstances in which the LLC may be dissolved.

An operating agreement is an internal document, and therefore one does not need to file it with the state. However, it should be updated every time there is a change in membership or management at the company. We recommend reading some samples of operating agreements (which can be easily found for free online) to find the best fit for your company.

Step Six: Get an EIN

As the last step, you will need to get an Employer Identification Number, or EIN, from the IRS. Also known as a Federal Tax Identification Number, your EIN is like a social security number for your LLC. An EIN is how the IRS tracks your business for tax purposes, but it is also necessary to open a business banking account and legally hire employees.

The good news is that EINs are free and can quickly be obtained by visiting the IRS.gov website.

To recap, these are the six steps to setting up an LLC on your own:

One: Choose your state
Two: Choose a name
Three: Nominate a registered agent
Four: File your articles of organization
Five: Create an Operating Agreement
Six: Get an EIN

When you have completed these steps, you will have an official LLC recognized at the state and federal level.

Congratulations!

Now that you have read and understood how to form an LLC, you might realize that you don't want to do it all by yourself. Fair enough. In that case, you might want to keep reading to understand how to best outsource the LLC creation process.

Hiring a Professional Service

The second way to form an LLC is nearly identical to the first, the only difference being that you pay a company to do for you all the steps mentioned above. There are many professional formation services for hire.

Service packages can involve many aspects of business formation, including drafting operating agreements, so you will have to choose based on your needs and budget.

The most important service that a professional offers, in addition to filing your articles of organization, is acting as your registered agent. This is the service that you most likely should consider using, even if you are filing all your paperwork yourself. Registered agent services typically have a fee ranging from 50 to 150 dollars. This is a small price to pay for the convenience and benefits provided by a professional service.

A hired registered agent helps you stay well-organized. In fact, it will keep your business mail separate and is available at all regular business hours to accept legal papers and official mail on your LLC's behalf. As we have already discussed above, an important additional benefit of using a registered professional agent is privacy. A professional service will provide a level of privacy by withholding your personal name and home address from the LLC's contact information.

There are many reasons you might not want your personal information easily accessible and associated with your business, and hiring a registered professional agent is an easy way to accomplish this.

Now that you have seen the different ways you can form an LLC take some time to research your options. Remember that every state has different laws and that many professional services are available to help you along the way.

17

Steps You Must Take After You Form an LLC

After you have registered your company as an LLC, you have to ensure that you handle everything properly. You want to make sure that your business is protected moving forward. In this chapter, we are going to go over all the things you need to do once you start your LLC to make sure your business runs smoothly.

Imagine you have just formed your LLC, and you are wondering what you have to do next. There are a number of things that you still need to take care of. The first two steps were already included in the previous chapter, but we give a little refresher.

Operating Agreement

We talked about this in detail in the previous chapter. While technically not mandatory in many states, we included drafting an operating agreement in the steps to take when forming an LLC. Having an operating agreement in place is, in fact, vital to make sure that if anything ever happens with your business, such as getting involved in a lawsuit, you have evidence that you are following the proper procedures. For instance, if one of your clients is trying to sue you, their attorney may use the lack of an operating agreement as evidence that, although the LLC has been formed, you are not actually operating as an LLC. This could put your personal assets at risk. Therefore, it is highly recommended to draft an operating agreement either during the formation of the LLC or immediately after.

Taxpayer Identification Number

Here is another step that we consider an integrating part of forming an LLC: Obtaining your EIN (Employer Identification Number). An EIN is essential since, without it, you cannot open a bank account for your business and start charging for your products or services.

Bank Account(s)

Once you have obtained your EIN, you need to open a bank account for the LLC. If, until now, you have been operating as a sole proprietorship and you are switching to an LLC, you must make sure that you transfer all the funds from your personal business account into the LLC bank account. Maintaining a clear separation between your personal bank account and your LLC bank account is fundamental.

Depending on the needs of your business, you might want to open up multiple bank accounts. Advantages of having multiple accounts include better security, better tracking of your business' cash flow, and the ability to draft a more accurate budget. Obviously, these pros must be weighed against the additional expenses of opening and maintaining several accounts.

Personal Business License

In case operating your business requires a personal business license or a permit, you would have to apply or reapply after forming your LLC. The license would be for you personally as an owner. For instance, if you want to form an LLC for your attorney business, you are required to have a privileged license from the licensing board in your state.

Vendor Contracts

You need to ensure that you have your contracts in place for your vendors, your clients, or any other business partners. If you switch from a sole proprietorship to LLC and you are still working with the same clients, you can simply change the business owner name in the contract to that of your LLC. It is important that when you sign those contracts, you have a legitimate signature.

When a member signs as a representative of the LLC, he or she should include language clarifying this. Otherwise (e.g., by simply signing with your name), you may invoke personal responsibility in corporate matters. A standardized signature block can help you avoid this type of confusion.

For instance, if Jane Doe signs on behalf of an LLC, she should clearly indicate that she is signing as a representative of the registered company and her relationship to the LLC. Here is what her signature on behalf of the LLC could look like:

Company X, LLC
   By: [*Jane Doe would add her signature here*]
   Jane Doe, President [*or simply "Managing Member"*]

Always remember to thoroughly read any document that you sign on behalf of the LLC, checking for sentences that could open you up to personal liability.

In case you already have contracts in place with vendors and clients, you must make sure to amend the old contracts with the new signature of the LLC.

18

Financing, Conversion, Dissolution

How to Fund an LLC

Before we start talking about how to fund your LLC, we must first clarify what it means to be a member of an LLC.

A member of an LLC is also known as an owner. Sometimes entrepreneurs contribute money to an LLC in order to acquire a share in the ownership of the company. However, it is important to note that you can be an owner of an LLC without actually investing any funds into it. In fact, you can contribute a service and still become a member (owner).

The bottom line is that you do not necessarily need to contribute capital to become an owner of an LLC. This is yet another instance of the extreme flexibility of LLCs: There are no rigid requirements to be an owner or member of an LLC except for being 18 years of age or older.

What is a capital contribution to your LLC?

A capital contribution is an amount that a member of an LLC allocates to the company itself to cover its initial expenses. These may include website design costs, personnel costs for the marketing and accounting team, renting an office, and so on.

The amount and type of such contributions can vary. While the majority of capital contributions are done in cash, a member can also make an initial capital contribution in the form of non-cash assets such as buildings and equipment.

After you have set up your LLC and the founding members have made their personal contributions to cover the initial expenses, you have three main ways of raising additional capital:

- **Equity contribution.** These are funds that are provided in exchange for a stake in the company. Anyone who makes an equity investment into an LLC becomes a member and has rights to the profits or losses of the company. These investments are the most attractive option to business owners since they provide funding that does not need to be repaid. Moreover, equity investments might bring into the company new members that are competent and motivated to make it succeed.
- **Debt investment.** This is money coming from investors who lend money to the LLC with the expectation that the loan will be paid back with interest. This is the most common form of capital for newly formed businesses. However, the company must back up these loans with some collateral. Therefore, a lack of collateral usually limits the amount of capital that can be acquired in this way.
- **Convertible debt.** This is just a combination of the previous two options. When the LLC takes on convertible debt, the company accepts a loan while agreeing to either pay back the money or convert the debt into equity at some time in the future.

It is important to remember that every person who buys equity into the company becomes a member and can participate in any type of member resolution that requires some form of voting. The new member must comply with a set of obligations and responsibilities that are outlined in the LLC operating agreement. Once again, we see how important it is for the operating agreement to be specific in describing each member's contributions, their percentage of ownership, as well as any sort of profit allocation. It should also be established in the agreement what happens if one of the members decides to leave the LLC.

Conversion: S Corp to LLC

An S Corp (S Corporation) is a corporate structure authorized by the Internal Revenue Code to transfer taxable income, credits, deductions, and losses directly to shareholders. The S Corp is a viable option only for small businesses with 100 or fewer shareholders and is similar in many respects to the limited liability company (LLC).

Both S Corps and LLCs are known as "pass-through entities" for tax purposes. Therefore, any income deductions or tax credits are passed through to the business owners and, thus, filed on those owners' individual tax returns. **There is no corporate tax return that must be filed for an LLC or S-corp.** For this reason, these two types of business structures avoid the issue of double taxation. In contrast, C corporations are subject to double taxation. The first taxation happens at the corporate level. Then, if the company passes on profit to its shareholders in the form of dividends, the shareholders must also report those dividends on their personal tax returns.

When should you convert from an S corp to an LLC?

As we have just seen, neither of these structures is taxed at the federal level. However, S corps are taxed on certain types of passive income. Since LLCs benefit from fewer formalities, simplified operations, and more flexible tax options, you may find it convenient to turn your S corp into an LLC.

For most types of businesses, LLCs are the best structure due to their simplicity, while adding a corporate status might needlessly complicate things. If you're not planning to sell stocks, or seek angel investor funding or venture capital, then you are probably better off as an LLC. An S corp structure, on the other hand, may be better for large, complex companies.

One of the first things you should be mindful of is that there are tax consequences for converting an S Corp to an LLC. It is important that you are aware of such tax implications, as they can heavily affect your business.

To successfully convert your company to an LLC, you will probably have to liquidate your S corp. For tax purposes, it is as if the corporation sold all of its assets. If the corp's assets have increased between the time of the formation of the business and the time of its conversion to an LLC, then capital gain is realized. Hence the shareholders will have to pay capital gains tax on the amount of that gain.

All this considered, it may still be appropriate to convert your business structure. Especially in the following circumstances:

The S-corp wants to create a liability shield. In most states, LLC members are shielded from creditors by what is called *charging order statutes.* Under a charging order, a creditor of the LLC can legally withhold money from distributions operated by the company until the debt is extinguished. However, a charging order does not provide the creditor with management rights in the LLC, nor can the creditor intervene in the running of the enterprise to which the debtor is a member. In most states, a charging order is the only way for the creditor of an LLC to recoup the money owed to them. Only in some states, the creditor can be authorized by the court to force the liquidation of the business to satisfy their claim against the debtor.

The S corp needs to liquidate assets ahead of time. We have seen that the S corp must liquidate assets if it is to be converted to an LLC. This could also be viewed as a benefit to a company that continues to grow exponentially. An S Corp that is experiencing massive and rapid growth might want to convert while the tax consequences of such liquidation are lower than at a later point. In fact, taxes would continue to increase based on the value of the assets to liquidate.

The S corp wants to bring in an inadmissible investor. It could be investor number 101 or a foreign citizen who is not a US resident. In these cases adding such "inadmissible" investors would cause the immediate termination of the S corporation. Transitioning to an LLC might be an appropriate way to bring in these investors.

In conclusion, choosing whether or not to convert an S-Corp to an LLC depends on your specific situation. Keep in mind that an LLC is one of the simplest business entities and structures to operate and manage. Based on your type of business, the number of members, and whether you have investors or not, you should evaluate if it is appropriate to convert your S Corp into an LLC.

Conversion: Sole Proprietorship to LLC

Many new entrepreneurs start out their businesses as sole proprietors. That is, they run a one-person enterprise in which there is no legal distinction between the owner and the business entity. To gain more financial control over their business as well as liability protection, they may wish at some point to transition from a Sole Proprietorship to an LLC.

If you have been operating a business as a sole proprietorship and you decide that, for liability reasons or tax purposes, you want to transition to an LLC, there is good news for you. In fact, the process that you will have to go through is not that different from just normally forming an LLC with a new business. First, you need to create an LLC. You can read more about the concrete steps you must take in the chapter of this book titled "How to Form an LLC." The main step is filing a document with your state's Secretary of State. Once you file the Articles of Organization or Certificate of Formation (the names of the documents vary from state to state) and they are approved, your LLC is formed.

Here are the additional points to consider when converting a sole proprietorship to an LLC.

The business name. If your sole proprietorship was operating under a trade name or a DBA and you want to continue operating under that DBA ("doing business as") with your LLC, then you will need to withdraw the current trade name registration and refile it with your LLC. If the name of the LLC is the same as your sole proprietorship's DBA, however, you don't need to worry about refiling the trade name. In this case, you will just operate under your LLC's name.

The EIN. Remember that one of the steps to undertake as soon as you have formed an LLC is to get an EIN (tax identification number) through the IRS. You may have had an EIN for your sole proprietorship if it had employees or if your bank required it, but now that you are changing to an LLC, it is mandatory that you get a new EIN since the LLC is a brand new entity. After getting the new EIN, you will have to update your bank account information so that it has the LLC's name and new tax ID number.

Permits and licenses. If your sole proprietorship was required to have any sort of permit or license to operate, you want to inquire whether you are required to add the name of your LLC on those documents.

Contracts. When converting from a sole proprietorship to an LLC, all the contracts must be amended to include the name of the newly formed LLC.

Dissolution

Dissolving an LLC simply means closing or shutting down your business. What are some of the most common reasons why business owners choose to dissolve their LLCs? The first one is to avoid paying the annual state renewal fees when they are no longer conducting business. The payment of these recurring fees keeps the LLC active. Even if your LLC stops operating, the state will continue to charge annual fees, and it may even add interest if they are not paid on time. The state will not let you officially dissolve the LLC until all outstanding taxes and fees have been paid in full. To avoid paying late fees, penalties, and interest fees, as well as to protect yourself from potential liabilities, it is important to officially dissolve your LLC the right way and in accordance with your state's requirements.

Ultimately, there is no need to be alarmed if your LLC has been inactive, but be sure not to wait too long to dissolve it.

How do you properly dissolve your LLC?

Generally, dissolving your business just involves filing a form to the business division of your state's secretary of state. The state may also require that you pay the state fee and send payments along with the dissolution documents. In some states, there is no charge, and in others, the fee can be hundreds of dollars. It is important to check with the business division at your secretary of state's office to find out the exact procedure.

Once you have taken the decision to dissolve your company, there are several steps to undertake to move things along, including notifying creditors, filing final tax returns, and informing all relevant government agencies. Here we summarize the most important points.

1. Vote to Dissolve the LLC

When members decide to dissolve the company, they take part in what is called voluntary dissolution. This can happen after they have cast a vote or because they are following the company's guidelines for events that automatically trigger dissolution, such as the death of a member. Refer to your LLC's operating agreement for proper procedures. In case your operating agreement does not address dissolution, you should follow the procedures described in your state's LLC laws.

After every member has voted and a majority agrees (or a cause for dissolution has occurred), make a record of this decision to dissolve the LLC and store it in the company's official records.

2. File Your Final Tax Return

In some states, you will have to obtain a tax clearance or good standing verification from the state tax agency before you can file the dissolution paperwork. Filing the final tax return and paying any taxes that are still due will satisfy this requirement. When you file the tax return for the company, be sure to indicate somewhere that this will be its last tax return. You will then receive authorization in the form of a certificate or letter from the IRS stating that you no longer have tax obligations.

Even if your state does not require a tax clearance, you still have to file your final tax return at both the state and federal levels, as well as the final employment tax return. Failing to do so might make you personally liable for unpaid payroll taxes.

3. File an Article of Dissolution

An article of dissolution is a document in which you ask the state to officially dissolve your LLC. You can find the form at your state's corporate division or on the Secretary of State's website. The form generally requires you to provide information about the company and its members and details about the company's assets and liabilities.

Once your article of dissolution has been approved and you have paid any processing fees, the state will send you a certificate of dissolution. Keep this important document in your files.

4. Settle Outstanding Debts

Even if your state might not require you to notify creditors before filing the dissolution deed, it is a good idea to do it anyway. In this way, you can pay all your company's obligations and reduce the possibility of unexpected claims arising in the future.

Creditors may include lenders, insurers, service providers, and suppliers. The notice should tell them a deadline for filing claims advising them that claims filed after the deadline will be barred. The appropriate deadline is set by your state's law, but it is usually between 90 and 180 days.

5. Distribute Assets

After you have paid your company's creditors as well as any outstanding taxes, all the remaining assets (including investments, profits, and tangible assets) can be distributed to the LLC owners. The operating agreement (or state law, if you do not have one) will set the terms of such distribution.

6. Conduct Wind Down Processes

Properly winding up the business includes several steps, such as firing employees, paying payroll taxes, canceling contracts, leases, business licenses, and permits, as well as notifying customers of the last date of business.

At the end of this process, you must close the company's bank accounts, federal employer identification number (FEIN), and state tax identification number, in case you have one.

In conclusion, if you are no longer using your LLC, then it is important to dissolve it. In this way, you can avoid getting hit with fees and potential interest payments. Be wary that some states will not let you officially dissolve the LLC until you pay everything that is owed to them.

19

How to Pay Yourself as an LLC

As the owner of an LLC, there are several different ways in which you can pay yourself.

Single-Member LLC

As a single-member LLC, the payment method is also known as *the draw of the owner*. Remember that the IRS considers single-member LLCs to be "disregarded entities." This means that the owner and business are one and the same thing when it comes to taxes. To be specific, your LLC profits will be treated as personal income instead of business income.

When you own a single-member LLC, you do not only use your Social Security Number for identification purposes. In addition, you are also identified with the EIN. You can apply for an EIN as soon as you form an LLC. It is mandatory to have one so that you can open up your business account. To avoid liability, you should be strict in separating your personal account from your business bank account.

When you transfer money from your business bank account to your personal account, you are taking a so-called *distribution*. You have simply distributed money to yourself. The company is passing business profits on to its owner.

This process is straightforward for a single-member LLC, but it can be more complex if you're part of a multi-member LLC. In that case, one needs to consider the operating agreement to understand how profits are allocated and at what frequency.

The main advantage of this system of distribution to pay yourself is its simplicity. However, the drawback is that you'll pay FICA, Medicare, and Social Security taxes (commonly called "self-employment tax") on all the revenue of your business instead of on only a fixed salary.

As a single-member LLC, your business does not receive a tax deduction when it writes you a check. This is because you are not processing payroll with a payroll company. When you pay your employees, you receive a deduction, but when you pay yourself, you receive no deduction.

One solution is to pay yourself as an employee. If you restrict yourself to what the IRS considers "reasonable compensation," then you can choose to be treated as an S-corporation for your taxes. The advantage of this system of paying yourself (as opposed to the distribution system) is that you only pay self-employment taxes on your salary instead of all business profits.

If you elect NOT to be treated as a corporation for tax purposes, then you are not restricted to a conventional salary. As the owner of a single-member LLC, you can pay yourself through distribution, also known as an "owner's draw." How much money and how often you draw is up to you, but ideally, you should leave sufficient funds in the corporate account to operate and grow the business.

Multi-Member LLC

Members of a multi-member LLC also use the owner's draw method to pay themselves. Each member can draw as many or as few shares as he or she wishes, as long as this complies with the company's operating agreement and sufficient funds remain for the daily costs and performance of the company.

If there are enough fund reserves, these LLCs can establish guaranteed payments for members. Analogous to salaries, guaranteed payments are paid regardless of the results of the business.

Corporate LLCs

Salaries and distributions

In case an LLC has chosen to be treated as an S corporation or a C corporation for tax purposes, its members (also called shareholders) are not allowed to take owner's draws. Instead, they are considered employees. Therefore, they must pay themselves a fixed salary on the company's regular payroll, with taxes deducted. This can be done using payroll software or by outsourcing the work to professionals.

As an LLC owner, you can determine the amount of your salary, but that amount must meet the requirements of "reasonable compensation." This is defined by the IRS as "the value that would normally be paid for similar services by similar businesses under similar circumstances."

In addition to your salary, you can also pay yourself distributions or dividends, which are distributions that come from a company's profit. Remember that distributions and dividends are considered taxable income.

20

Common LLC Mistakes You Can Easily Avoid

Although limited liability companies offer protection to the business owner, and many entrepreneurs form an LLC to shield their personal assets from confiscation in the case of a lawsuit, there are instances when your personal assets are at risk.

What are the risks?

Piercing the veil

What is piercing the veil?

Veil piercing is a means by which courts ignore the separate existence of the LLC. Since the entity is no longer there, the business owner becomes liable for the debts of the company.

Breaking the veil can be an issue for companies regardless of how big they are. However, the most common case is for a corporation or LLC with one or a few owners when it is not capable of paying its debt. Usually, the creditor sues the corporation or LLC for the outstanding payment. Once that happens, the LLC has to pay off the debt. If that still does not happen, the creditor ends up suing the business owners and asks the court to "pierce the veil" to hold the business owners personally liable.

To ensure the best possible protection for your personal assets, you should avoid these common mistakes made by LLC owners:

Not writing an operating agreement

We have already discussed the details contained in the operating agreement. For instance, how the LLC is run, plans to buy a property or other assets for the company, how you and the other members are paid, what start-up investments you and the other member will contribute to the enterprise, what type of business activity the company is engaged in, potential insurance, licenses, and permits that are required to run the business, where the business is located, and finally what happens in case the company is dissolved. It is crucial that you include in the operating agreement any relevant information that defines the business. This can appear an overwhelming task, as there are a lot of details. However, an operating agreement helps identify your business as an entity separate from yourself in case of a lawsuit. A detailed and professionally compiled operating agreement adds a further layer of protection, making it unlikely that your personal affairs get mixed up with your business affairs.

Not recording meeting minutes

This step is not strictly required for LLCs. However, we strongly recommend you record minutes every time a meeting is held. You should aim to conduct a meeting with all the members at least once every year. Carefully record the place, date, and time where the meeting took place. Write down any change in the membership structure or in the business model and major investments or acquisitions in which the company has been involved during that year. Keep these notes (the so-called *meeting minutes*) in a folder together with all the important documents related to your LLC. Even if your company is a Single-Member LLC, you can still write meeting minutes. If this is your situation, it will be more of an annual report in which you discuss the evolution of your business during the last 12 months. Once again, having a collection of reports of this kind is useful to establish that the company is being run properly as an entity separate from you as an individual.

No bookkeeping

The third most common mistake of LLC owners is not doing proper book-keeping. It is fundamental to track and keep a record of any expense or revenue generated by the LLC. If you do that, you will have a much easier time when you have to file your taxes. Make sure your bookkeeping is also timely. Do not postpone the recording of revenues or expenses but go ahead and do it as soon as possible. This will lower the risk of forgetting to record some transactions. Clear and transparent bookkeeping records will help you justify your balances in case of a tax audit. An online service such as Quickbooks can be extremely helpful in tracking your monthly revenue and expenses.

Not having a business account

As we have seen before, one of the first steps you should take after forming your LLC is opening a bank account for your business. This is necessary if you want to keep your finances and those of your business separate. If you don't have a separate account for your business, it will be easier to pierce the corporate veil when you are involved in litigation. Remember that to open a business bank account, you need your EIN number. Make sure you read the chapter called "How to Pay Yourself as an LLC" if you want to learn more about the ways in which you can operate transactions from the LLC's bank account to your personal account.

Not financing your LLC properly

If you operate too many transactions between the LLC's account and your personal bank account, then the corporate veil will become easier to pierce during litigation. Make sure at all times that the company's account has enough money to handle a few months of operating expenses. In this way, you will avoid having to constantly transfer money into it from your personal account. This may seem a common sense action, but the truth is that many new LLC owners have the tendency to withdraw money from the company's account as soon as it is deposited.

Signing contracts with your own name

Avoid signing rental contracts or any other type of contract with your name instead of the name of the LLC. For instance, if you are leasing new office space, write the LLC as the entity to which the space is being rented and then sign the documents with your personal signature as the owner of the LLC.

Confusing personal funds and business funds

The only transactions between your personal bank account and that of the LLC should involve funding your business and paying yourself. You should avoid using your LLC's bank account for non-business purposes, for instance, making personal car payments or internet subscriptions for strictly personal use (e.g., Netflix).

Not having any liability insurance

Having some sort of insurance is always recommended since it adds further protection to your personal and company assets. In case of a lawsuit, the insurance company will cover the amount established in your insurance policy.

The alter ego doctrine

The protection and shielding offered by the LLC are not all-encompassing. In court, the following question will be raised. "Is the LLC just an *alter ego* of its owner, or is it a truly separate entity?" If you make any of the mistakes described above, then the LLC might be regarded as your *alter ego* during litigation. The court will declare an "alter ego" case if the LLC lacks a separate identity. Establishing the presence of an *alter ego* enables the court to pierce the veil and therefore hold the owners personally responsible for the company's debts.

The bottom line is that you should aim to create the highest degree of separation between you and your company. Keep in mind that abiding by the formalities normally reserved for corporations adds more layers of protection between the LLC and your personal assets.

21

LLC Glossary

Annual Report — A document that needs to be filed every year. It provides information, such as past performance, financial condition, or business objectives of the limited liability company.

Articles of Organization — The name of the document that needs to be filed in some states to form a limited liability company.

Certificate of Good Standing — A certificate, also called certificate of existence, that serves as evidence for the existence of a limited liability company. It is typically issued by a state official. The certificate authorizes the company to conduct business.

Conversion — Changing your current business structure to a new business structure (e.g., Conversion of an S corp to an LLC).

Corporation — A large company or family of companies created and authorized to act as a single entity.

Dissolution — Dissolving an LLC simply means closing or shutting down its business. By dissolving your LLC, you ensure that you no longer have to pay your annual LLC fees and business taxes or file annual reports.

Distribution — The transfer of money of property by a limited liability company to a member.

Domestic LLC – An LLC is domestic in the state where it is created and foreign everywhere else.

Employer Identification Number (EIN) — A means of identification from the Internal Revenue Service (IRS). Also known as a Federal Tax Identification Number, your EIN is like a social security number for your LLC. An EIN is how the IRS tracks your business for tax purposes, but it is also necessary to open a business banking account and legally hire employees.

Foreign LLC — Despite the name, it does not mean that the company comes from another country. Instead, it means your business was organized under the laws of a different state.

Holding Company — A holding company, or umbrella company, is a parent business entity, that is, a corporation with subsidiaries. These subsidiaries are separate businesses that are wholly or partially owned by the parent.

Liability Insurance — An insurance that helps protect your company in case of a lawsuit. It may protect from various liability claims (e.g., employee injury, damage to the property of others).

Limited Liability Company — An entity incorporated under the Limited Liability Company law of a state. It is a hybrid business structure that contains both characteristics of a corporation and of a partnership.

Managers — The individuals selected by the LLC members to be in charge of the daily operations of an LLC.

Meeting Minutes — A written record of all the votes, discussions, and steps that occurred during an LLC meeting.

Members — The owners of a limited liability company.

Multi-member LLC — An MMLLC has multiple owners. These can be individuals, other LLCs, or corporations. Although technically, an MMLLC can have an arbitrary number of members, the most popular type is a two-member LLC for businesses run by a husband/wife couple or by two friends who act as partners.

Operating Agreement — The document that provides the basic rules for the conduct of the business and partnerships of the limited liability company. It also contains information on the relationship between business owners and managers.

Signature LLC — The signature of an LLC is different from that of a sole proprietorship in that it clearly defines the line of responsibility. Therefore, the first line of the signature should contain the name of the LLC, followed by the role (e.g., acting president, business owner, manager) and the name of the particular person whose role was previously mentioned.

Single-Member LLC — A single-member limited liability company has only one owner or member. That individual bears the full responsibility of the company, including being accountable for tax payments.

Sole Proprietorship — An unincorporated business that has only one business owner.

Voting Rights — Members' rights to be involved in the affairs of the company. According to their own interest, they make decisions on all issues that pertain to the business.

22

LLC FAQ

What documents do I need to file to form an LLC?

When you form an LLC, you need to file various legal documents. The following documents are required to register your company as an LLC:

- **Name Reservation Application** —As the name says, the Name Reservation Application is used to reserve a name for your LLC. Keep in mind that some states may have restrictions regarding the permissibility of a name and that the chosen name must be available.
- **Articles of Organization** — It must be filed through the Secretary of State. You can download the form from the website of the Secretary of State.
- **An operating agreement** —It contains regulations related to how the business should be run. It includes the rights of the members and information on relationships between managers and members of the organization.

Note: Depending on your location, you may not be required to file all of the above-mentioned documents.

Who is liable for LLC debt?

The liable entity for an LLC's debt is the LLC itself. Creditors can only go after the assets held by the LLC unless one of the LLC's members personally co-signed a business loan, put up their own property as collateral, committed fraud, or if the LLC's corporate veil has been pierced. The corporate veil is the phrase used to describe the limited liability protection that forming an LLC gives its owners. When you form an LLC, your personal assets, such as your house or your car, will not be on the line if your business is sued. Nevertheless, the corporate veil has its limits. LLC owners need to take steps to make sure that their corporate veil does not get pierced. For instance, they need to ensure that they do not mix their business and personal finances, have enough capital to cover their liabilities, sign business documents on behalf of the LLC, document company affairs, or maintain the LLC's good standing with the state.

What happens if my LLC is inactive?

Due to illness, I abandoned my LLC a few years back. I am sure I received requests from the state, but I bravely ignored them. I am a little more nervous now - how should I address this, if at all? I did nothing with it, and I made no income.

Many states will dissolve LLCs after a certain period of time if the LLC does not remain compliant (i.e., they fail to file an annual report). LLCs that fail to file their annual report with the state may lose their good standing and may end up dissolved or forfeited. If you want to revive an LLC, you will have to contact the state for the reinstatement package. If your LLC has remained compliant, it will remain active until you file a certificate of dissolution.

Can an LLC have an unlimited life?

Thanks to recent changes to the IRS tax code, LLCs can now be created without setting a dissolution date, therefore allowing them to have potentially unlimited life.

What is the difference between "Managers" and "Members" in an LLC?

Members of an LLC are similar to stockholders of corporations. In fact, a synonym for "members" is "owners." They own a piece of the company based on the value of their initial investment. Managers, instead, are people chosen by the members to coordinate, run, and manage the day-to-day operations of the company. A manager may or may not be a member of the LLC.

Is an LLC required to hold meetings?

One of the main advantages of an LLC is that it has fewer formal requirements than a corporation. One of them is having regular meetings. When forming an LLC, you can state in your operating agreement whether you want to hold meetings and with which frequency. Not requiring meetings results in less paperwork and, therefore, a lower risk of not complying with the law.

How much is the cost of forming and operating an LLC?

In certain states, you may be required to pay an annual fee when you file your annual report. In addition, depending on your location, you may have to pay state taxes.

In some states, you will be subject to annual fees for your LLC. Here are some examples of states and the LLC costs that you would incur in those states:

California: In California, you would have to pay a $20 reporting fee. This payment must be made as soon as you file an LLC, as well as every two years afterward (i.e., as long as your LLC is still operating). Furthermore, you would have to pay an $800 LLC tax. This tax fee is due every year on the 15th day of the fourth month that the LLC was registered. Keep in mind that this is a recurring annual fee. If your LLC's income is higher than $250,000, it may owe further state tax.

Nevada: In Nevada, you must pay a $150 fee for the Initial List of Members and Managers. In addition, you would have to pay a $200 fee for Business license registration and renewals. The Business license application fee must be paid within the first month of filing the LLC. No state taxes must be paid in Nevada.

Delaware: The only fee that LLCs must pay in Delaware is an annual fee of $300. It has to be paid each year on June 1 after the LLC has been formed.

New York: In New York, it is mandatory to have publications of news about the LLC in two newspapers in the county where the LLC is registered. Publication fees can be as high as $2000. As soon as the publication is done, the company must pay a $50 filing fee and submit to the state a certificate of publication.

What are some differences between an S-Corporation and an LLC?

S-corporations and LLCs are very similar, but there are a few important differences. An LLC has fewer restrictions and more flexibility in the running of its operation. Some of the restrictions of an S-corporation are being limited to one class of stock and not being permitted more than 100 stockholders. There are also important differences between the two business structures when it comes to taxes. Owners of an LLC are required to pay self-employment taxes on all of their profits, while S-corporation shareholders do not have to pay taxes on anything above their annual salary (as long as this is considered by the IRS to be "reasonable compensation"). Remember that an LLC can also elect to be treated as an S corp for tax purposes (see the chapter "How to pay yourself as an LLC").

When I file articles of organization or amendment, how many copies do I need to send?

Only one. Send two copies only if the filer wants a copy bearing the filing stamp.

IV

Book 4: The Complete Marketing Handbook

23

What is Marketing?

Marketing is broadly defined as the action of promoting and selling products or services. It involves many steps, from the initial market research to the actual advertising. Marketing is essential in starting and growing a successful business, and therefore you must **make it a priority and not an afterthought**. It is not uncommon for new companies to get started and be ready to distribute their products or services, only to realize that they do not know how to sell them.

It is a common mistake to believe that marketing is just the last step, something you can start thinking about when the product is ready to be sold. Abandon that false idea. Successful marketing begins with careful research in human behavior, which must be conducted even before developing your product. The moment you have a business idea and are trying to make it concrete, you must ask yourself: *Is this something people want? Is there a demand for this product?* Market research is crucial to answer those questions and make sure that your product is the right one. Go out there, conduct surveys, study the market, and use all the data available online and in newspapers. **Identify your target audience, and when you have profiled it, build your product around them.** Have marketing in mind from the very first day you start working on your idea, and let it accompany and guide every step of the production.

In today's world, it is not enough to build the best product or even the perfect product for your audience. Why? Because nobody will buy it unless they know about it. You need to ensure the public is aware of what you have to offer. That is why, **at the beginning of your business activity, you should spend half of your time on marketing**. We have seen in the previous chapter that by positioning your product appropriately in a market segment, you attach a message to it. Now it is the job of marketing to make sure that that message reaches your potential clients.

Marketing is more than just creating a logo for your company and attractive packaging for your product. Especially for someone operating on a low budget (as you will be doing at the beginning), it involves being present online with an attractive website and having engaging profiles on social media. It also involves interacting with your customers and replying to their questions and reviews. Again, to understand how to do all this effectively, extensive market research is necessary: you first need to profile the target audience of your marketing campaign. Consider your potential customers and find out the answers to the following questions. Who are they? What is their median age? Why are they interested in buying what you have to offer? What are their motivations and needs? How would they buy your product, in a store or online? Will they buy more at a specific time of the year? And so on.

Before getting into the details of the different aspects of marketing and market research, let us discuss what I consider to be the three most important points that you should keep in mind when formulating your marketing strategy.

Marketing Advice #1: **Focus on your social media presence**. On average, small business owners spend six hours weekly marketing on social media. This average is even higher among new entrepreneurs. It is no mystery that young people are very fond of social media and often know the ins and outs of all the different platforms. Most business owners try to occupy every corner of the social media world, to be present everywhere. You can find countless online articles advising young entrepreneurs to be on every platform, even recommending a minimum number of posts per day for each platform. However, as research shows, that approach is totally misguided.

Here is a lesson from the experience of many entrepreneurs: *if you are everywhere, you are nowhere.* When you start from scratch or are still at the small business level, you have no energy or power to infiltrate every platform. You can be in all of them, but your presence will be too sporadic and superficial, unable to make a difference. How often are you going to answer messages in one platform if you are trying to manage six of them? (Apart from everything else you must do to actually run your business). **It is better to concentrate your efforts on a couple of places or even on only one platform** and become really effective there.

Remember that as a new business, you will have an incredibly hard time building your trust and credibility. So, how are you going to do it? Here is the answer: **become a strong, reliable presence on one platform**. If you spread yourself too thin trying to manage many different social media, you will end up achieving nothing. Build one single profile, but do it well and professionally, uploading high-quality pictures and videos to make a great first impression. Respond timely to messages and try to interact with pages and communities whose members are potentially interested in your product. Do all this well on one platform. There will be a time when you will be present everywhere, but that time has not arrived yet.

Here are two more tips for you:

- Always keep in mind that you are advertising a business, not trying to become an influencer. Therefore, don't waste your time. Limit your engagement with your audience to discussions focused on what you have to offer. Again, **you are selling a product, not hunting for followers.**
- Make sure you have a way of gathering emails to stay in touch with your

potential customers.

- Choose the platform you are going to tackle based on customer research. Do your potential customers hang out on Instagram, or do they prefer Facebook or maybe Pinterest? On which platform do you find your competitors?

If you follow these strategies, you will already have an advantage since the social media presence of most small companies is highly disorganized and ineffective.

Marketing Advice #2: Believe in your product. One of the cornerstones of marketing is the product itself. It should be something you like, or better, something you love. You must want people to buy it because you sincerely believe it's great. You must have a high level of commitment to your product. After all, if you are not convinced yourself, how can you aspire to convince your customers? Here is the bottom line: **develop and sell something you value and care about**.

Why is this so crucial? Let me answer with an analogy. I have always wanted to play the piano. Without that deep passion and commitment, I would never have had the patience to endure endless hours of practicing scales. It can get extremely repetitive and, therefore, boring. **Marketing is based on repetition**. Have you ever wondered why you keep seeing the same commercial on TV or hearing the same spot on the radio, sometimes even multiple times within just a few minutes? Why do they bother to broadcast the same ad again after such a short time? The answer is that it needs to pass in front of your eyes or reach your ears many times before your mind really notices it. Your mind gets the message only through repetition. (We will discuss more in detail later the science behind this "mere exposure effect"). The bottom line is that you must truly love what you are selling, or you will soon get sick of it.

If you are serious about marketing, you cannot be polite. "Oh, I already posted this ad on that group yesterday; maybe I shouldn't post it again." If you think like this, you are on the wrong track. You must be bold, believe in your product, and stand behind it. Do you know that feeling when as a child, you are all excited about a drawing you have made, and you want to show it to everyone and can't stop talking about it? That is the level of excitement you need to reach for the product or service you are selling. With that motivation, you will find the willpower to pursue a relentless and effective marketing strategy that will put you on the right track to success.

Marketing Advice #3: **Dominate your niche**. Remember what was said regarding your social media presence: being everywhere means being nowhere. The same applies to advertising in general. A brand of luxury cars doesn't target the middle class, a company producing skiing equipment doesn't sell in the Bahamas, and a videogame store won't advertise to elderly people. Of course, it is possible that your grandpa wants to buy a console, but it is unlikely that he was the target of a marketing campaign for that product. Have you ever seen an ad for a private jet? Probably not. That means the marketers of that company are doing their job properly. That commercial would have been wasted on you since you most likely could not afford such a vehicle. **While potentially everyone can buy a product, no product is marketed to everyone**. Let me say that again: no company is trying to sell a product to *everyone* indiscriminately. So why should you?

On the contrary, find your own niche, customize your offer, and distinguish your product from the ones offered by the competition. Don't worry about specializing too much. Even big corporations that are now involved in literally anything were born as niche industries. Can you guess which company started as an online marketplace for books, later expanded to sell electronics, software, video games, apparel, furniture, food, toys, and jewelry, and nowadays even offers cloud computing, digital streaming, and artificial intelligence?

It is impossible to please everyone. Your product, at least at the beginning, will not be of interest to most people. Who cares. Do not make the mistake of going for a one-size-fits-all company. You need to know exactly whose needs you are catering to, make the best possible product for your target audience, and try to reach them with your message. Your goal should be to get to the top of your niche. Once you are in that position of dominance, you will be ready to conquer other segments of the market.

Let us now dive deeper into all the main aspects of marketing.

24

The 4Ps of Marketing and Selling

The path to a great marketing strategy can't be defined by a single element. You must evaluate your product, how customers interact with the product, and how they interact with your marketing efforts.

All these factors create a "marketing mix" that shows you how to appropriately market your product to your audience. Shape your "marketing mix" by evaluating the four Ps: product, place, price, and promotion.

Product (or Service). If you are trying to market a new product, you must first consider the product itself. Ask yourself the following questions about the product so you can get a better idea of how to promote it to your customers:

- How will this product benefit our customers?
- How is the product different from other products on the market?
- What advantages should we promote, and which disadvantages should we be prepared to defend?
- What features of the product are most appealing to customers?

Get a really good idea of your product and what you're offering is the first step.

Place. To make a purchase, customers will need access to your product. Placing your product and marketing content requires more strategy than you may think. Social media and the internet have vastly expanded the ways that customers can search for products, find reviews, and make the final purchase. Ask yourself the following questions about where to place your product:

- Where do our customers look for information?
- Where do they look to make a purchase?
- How have online retail and e-commerce changed the way customers look for our product?
- What online or brick-and-mortar trends should we pay attention to?
- What social media platforms or online resources do our customers use and trust?

Placing is important because how in the world are your customers going to buy your product or service or find out more? The place can be a domain, a storefront, or even an app.

Price. If you think first and foremost about profits, numbers, and prices, you may have skipped ahead and thought about your prices first. The price that you assign to your product may change or vary depending on the place or time when customers see the product. Prices can be made more appealing through many different strategies, including discounting or anchoring, which we will discuss in detail in later chapters. Before you stick a price tag on your product, ask the following questions

- What do our customers think is a fair price for our product?
- What do our competitors price similar products at, and how can we use those prices to our advantage?
- How will changes, discounts, or trial offers affect our customers' perception of our original price?

You really do need to think a lot about the value you're selling and the price point you're setting for your customers.

Promotion. Promoting your product can be the biggest headache of the 4 Ps. You know the ins and outs of your product but sending an effective message that leads your customers to the checkout line isn't always obvious. Social media and the internet have expanded the ways that brands promote their products and the way customers expect to be sold to. Consider the following answers when you are creating your strategy:

- Where and when are the best times to begin to promote your product?
- What channel (or a mix of channels) will reach your audience at each stage of the buyer's journey?
- What messages will help to promote your product effectively?

When you ask yourself the above questions, consider the other Ps and elements that play into reaching your customers with an effective and convincing message. If, for example, you are promoting your product with a message and price that appeals to customers, but your message is placed where none of your customers will see it, you won't land any sales.

If you search for the four Ps online, you may find some additional Ps in your results. The truth is, as marketing strategy has adapted to social media and new technology, so have the four Ps. In addition to the basic four Ps above, consider the following Ps when you are creating your strategy. These four Ps are commonly applied to copywriting and content creation.

Promise. A customer-centric approach to marketing requires you to answer the following question: "How will this benefit your customers?" When you are marketing your product or brand to customers, you have to make your value, and your promises known straight away. Communicate your promises effectively to draw in your customers with an email subject or a tweet. In video marketing, I might start by saying, "In this video, you're going to learn the 8Ps of marketing, something that nobody has ever revealed in a single video before" That's the promise of the content.

Picture. Facts and figures get lost online and pushed aside by more engaging and colorful content. Paint a picture and craft a story to customers about how a product will benefit their lives. Use engaging and exciting content to show, not tell, customers about how they can use the product and how it will be the answer to their needs or problems. Appeal to their emotions before you create your call to action. (For more information on how this can be done on social media, skip to our chapter on social media marketing.) In this chapter, I could say to you, "What if you could use the 8Ps to create jaw-dropping content that hooked your customers, and more than half of them immediately handed over their wallets? At the end of the day, you drive home in your fancy sports car to your huge humble mansion and fall asleep with notifications of happy customers." If your market is 18-34 males, you're really painting a picture that a lot of that demographic desires, and you can then move on to the next P.

Proof. The emotional language will draw in an expressive customer, but more analytical customers want hard facts in addition to a great story. How does your customer know that your product is going to do what you say it will? Where's the proof? The proof is in customer testimonials, stats, awards, etc. Adding these types of proof builds trust and shows your customers that you can back up the picture you are painting for them. If you do not have this proof to share, it's time to reach out to former customers and set other strategies into place so you can brag about the value of your brand in your marketing content. I could say, "I've sold millions of dollars using the 4Ps and have actually trained over 300 other salespeople to use the same technique, totaling over 4 billion in sales in the past year alone." And that'd be perfect proof that what I know and what I teach has credibility.

Pitch (aka Push). Once you have led your customer through the buyer's journey with a good mix of emotive language and hard proof of your value, it's time to make a final push with your sales pitch. How are you going to close the sale? How can you confirm interest in not only the product but also the purchase? These final pushes should only be distributed once other marketing content has been sent out and received by customers. Pitches will be more effective once you have established that the customer is interested in continuing through the buyer's journey with you and your business. You can use every trick in this book to lock them down and secure the sale at this point.

We have mentioned that a mixture of many different Ps will show you the best way to create a customized marketing strategy that will reach your specific audience. Consider the following examples of how the four Ps interact with each other to reach more customers and close more sales: A landscaping company is trying to promote a new service: backyard lighting installation. They craft a blog post on their company website called "10 Creative Ways to Decorate Your Backyard." The blog post is written so it can be placed as the top result for customers who Google searches like "how to decorate a backyard" or "decorate backyard with lighting." Or maybe they go viral on Pinterest, which in my experience, would be very easy to do with this topic.

The blog post paints a picture of a beautifully lit backyard that can help customers entertain guests and keep their property safe in the nighttime. At the end of the blog post, the blog post promotes lighting installation services. Without making too much of a push, the post invites readers to sign up for a mailing list (with the promise of more information) or contact the company for a free consultation from a landscaping expert. The blog post is on the company's website, which interested customers can explore. Additional landing pages explain the benefits of the product in further detail, as well as the price. Throughout the page, the customer can find testimonials and other forms of proof that the brand is trustworthy and its products are worth the investment. Adding a blog post to your company website puts your product in front of potentially interested customers and gives them the option to explore further and continue along the buyer's journey.

The structure of the website, including calls-to-action and the placement of testimonials, are all shaped by the Ps mentioned in this chapter. When you are creating content and your overall marketing strategy, keep the four Ps (and additional Ps of content creation) in mind.

25

Market Research: How to Ask the Right Questions

Navigating the customer journey and each buyer persona can be a headache, but an in-depth knowledge of your audience is necessary to lead them from a stranger to a loyal supporter of your brand. Asking the right questions and taking on the qualities of a naturally curious person can help you build an effective marketing strategy and give your sales a big boost.

A good set of questions can open the doors to a productive conversation or can awkwardly shut one down. Asking open-ended questions, and responding with active listening, give you the best chance at getting the answers you need to pitch your products effectively. Let's start with open-ended questioning. An open-ended question is something that requires more than a "yes" or "no" answer.

For example, "Are you looking for a new car?" is a close-ended question. The customer could answer, "no," and then the conversation stops short. A better open-ended question is, "What are you looking for in a new car?"

An open-ended question gives the customer more to talk about and more information for you to make tailored suggestions and offer tailored solutions to their needs. If you are having trouble asking questions after you've received an initial answer, use this type of questioning to get the ball rolling and the conversation flowing.

Start with an open-ended question. The question may be, "What are you looking for in our products?" or "How do you see our company benefiting your business?" When the customer gives you an answer, take a piece of their answer and question it further. If the answer is, "I am looking for a car that has a high safety rating for my family and me," ask a further question about their family. If the answer is, "I am looking to expand my business in the next five years," ask further questions about what markets or demographics they are looking to expand in.

This type of questioning gives you an easy follow-up question and shows the customer that you are listening to what they are saying. Active listening builds trust and helps you make the best suggestions for your customers in terms of products and solutions to their needs. After a while, you may begin to hear the same answers over and over. These similar answers shape a buyer's persona and help you get to know your customer base better.

Once you have enough experience with these questions, you will be able to know the answers, and find the best solutions for your customers, faster. Studies show that people who are genuinely curious about an answer are more likely to remember it. Stay engaged with your customers, and you will find that their answers are more common than you might think, and at some point, they will become completely predictable to you.

If you want to take on the qualities of a curious person to get to know your customers better and benefit your sales, here are the secret ingredients:

Creativity. Constantly churning out questions and solutions for customers can be exhausting, but it is necessary to stand out and close a sale. With so much information and content being sent around smartphones and social media, creativity will grab your customers' attention before your competitors do. An outstanding question, whether it's in an email subject line or over the phone, or on a Facebook ad, can be enough to stop a customer in their tracks and get them to focus their attention on you. Creativity is also necessary if you want to keep trudging forward and learn more about your customers than just the two or three questions you've memorized before they walked in the door.

Focus. Active listening and following through on your curiosity requires focusing on the present moment and the task at hand. Staying focused also helps to build trust with customers. Active curiosity shows customers that you are treating them as if they are individuals with unique needs, not just another sale.

Positivity. One of the reasons curious people ask further questions is that they are optimistic and excited to know more about the situation at hand. A positive attitude comes in from the moment you meet a customer to the moment you close a sale or receive feedback on why the sale didn't go through. Rejection is all too common in the world of sales (although it can be handled with grace, with tips from our Objection Handling chapter.) Stay positive and stay curious!

Passion. Passion and positivity go hand in hand. When customers see that you are determined to help them find the product or solution of their dreams, they are more willing to trust you. Curiosity is more than just asking the question; it's being invested in the answer and learning more about your customers. Treat each question as if it will add value to your sales (because it will!)

Willingness to Collaborate. The right answer isn't always in a direct sale or an answer that you provide. A truly curious person will expand their thinking and open their mind to a wider collaboration. Two heads are better than one; those two heads could be you and your customer, you and a fellow coworker, or you and anyone who can help you close a sale to help serve your customer.

Ability to Take Feedback. You shouldn't just ask questions about the customer to make a sale. After an interaction or sale, asking questions about your performance or the overall experience can give you important feedback. Continue to be curious and follow through with each customer, no matter what the end result may be. If you did not close the sale, curiosity and openness can tell you what you should do differently to close the next sale.

Stay curious and keep asking questions until you (and your customer) find the answers you need to close a sale. Customer research should be an exercise in curiosity and creativity and a place where you can exercise all your personal qualities.

26

Attaching a Message to Your Brand

Customers aren't always just looking for one single quality in your products, and you may have more to give them than you can fit in a sentence. When you are trying to reach a large audience that pays attention to many different messages, it can be easy to throw out a lot of different content. **Trying to tick every box and appeal to everyone has good intentions, but often comes off as confusing** to customers who are reading content in different tones that are sending mixed messages. To build trust and keep buyers with you throughout the customer journey, you must **be consistent**.

Whether you are telling someone in your household to do the dishes or telling a customer how great your products are, you probably must tell them more than once. There are so many messages and advertisements, and information sources out in our world, so remembering something that you've heard for the first time is becoming less and less common. Advertisers know the **rule of 7.** Customers typically must hear a message seven times before they take action to make a purchase. The great value of your products or the great reviews from your customers may fall on deaf ears if they are only communicated once or twice. Even if you or your team feels like a broken record, repetition and consistency are easier to remember.

Your message is more likely to stick with your customers if it is consistent and repeated throughout social media, advertisements, or face-to-face interactions. The same goes for the way your website is designed or the products that you highlight. The color scheme is an easy way to consistently display your brand. If your business card looks radically different from your company website, customers may be confused as to whether they have the right website address. Inconsistency halts the process of building trust and communicating with your customer by confusing them.

We all know that Wal-Mart is known for its cheap products. If they start advertising themselves solely as a business that has a clean store or that sells fresh produce, readers and customers may be confused. Both things could be true but are not consistent with Wal-Mart's main message.

You want your content to clearly separate you from your competition. If your content and your message are even just a little confusing and do not revolve around one clear message, your customers will have a harder time picking you over your competition because they do not know what to expect.

Consistency is important throughout your content and every interaction in the customer journey. Every person that is part of your business, technical support and advertisers alike, should know your top values and how to communicate them to customers. If your content boasts a positive message, but your customer support representatives are grumpy and negative, your customers will feel as though you have let them down. Consistency creates expectations for your products, your employees, and the purchase itself. If you can consistently communicate to your customers that your products are of great value, they will have confidence in their purchase and continue to hold your company to the standards that you have set.

Customers who see a consistent message will have a better understanding of what to expect from your business and what they should expect when they initially make a purchase. Consistent messages in sales can also help to **show you and your team what works and what does not work** to close sales and build a loyal customer base. Using a consistent message throughout a marketing campaign can help you see how that message reaches customers from its initial launch until the next marketing campaign begins. If you are sending out mixed messages during a campaign, it will be hard to measure what resonated with customers and what turned them off.

A consistent message will help you create an even better campaign or sales interaction in the future. You should aim for consistency even when performing A/B testing. If, for example, you are testing email subject lines, you may only need to tweak one or two words to understand what your customers respond to more. Individual words can be changed; after all, content must be adjusted to social media audiences and the size of your platform. **Your overall message, however, needs to reflect the same handful of core values or product benefits** that the customer will grasp once they have seen it a few times.

Before you start any marketing campaign, think of your customer avatar, and ask yourself the following questions:

- What is the one important message you want to get across to your prospects?
- How do you make all your marketing efforts consistent with this core message?

27

Getting Exposure

Sometimes, all it takes for a product to appeal to customers is for it to be present in their minds. Simply putting products in front of customers may seem like too simple of a tactic to work, but the **mere exposure theory** offers evidence that this tactic is more effective than we might think.

The "mere exposure effect" (also known as the familiarity principle or the exposure effect) is the theory that people are more positive toward things that they recognize. Simply recognizing something - whether it is a person, phrase, or object - is enough to make it more favorable or trustworthy.

This effect takes place as a feeling before it takes place as a conscious thought. The mere exposure effect works, despite our first impressions. If a new product is introduced on the market, it will only gain favor as we see it in our everyday lives. If we see or hear something that is unfavorable at first, the mere exposure effect assures us that familiarity will soften the negative feelings we have. Studies have shown that, eventually, enough exposure to something will turn our feelings from negative to neutral or even positive.

The mere exposure effect was popularized by social psychologist Robert Zajonc. In "The Attitudinal Effects of Mere Exposure," Zajonc conducts four different experiments. In one, people were shown illustrations that were meant to look like Chinese characters. Participants were told that each character represented an adjective and asked participants to guess whether the represented word was positive or negative. The characters that were shown to participants more often were perceived to represent more positive words.

In 1967, an experiment was conducted by Professor Charles Goetzinger at Oregon State University. Every Monday, Wednesday, and Friday, a student wearing only a full-body black bag and shoes would come to the class. The student's identity was known only to Goetzinger. At first, students did not respond positively to the student wearing the bag. By the end of the semester, however, Goetzinger noticed that the class was more friendly to the student in the bag.

The mere exposure effect is the idea that has driven product placement in movies and television. Based on the idea of mere exposure, product placement should be a simple way to advertise brands and products. Research (and general experience with product placement in media) shows that product placement is best done subtly. Product placement that is too obvious is often viewed as obnoxious by consumers who do not want to feel like they are being tricked into buying.

In general, sales teams and advertisers should consider strategy before basing advertisements or messages on the mere exposure effect. Proper research and measurement are necessary to make sure that the theory is working to generate leads and close sales.

A simple theory like mere exposure isn't always simple to implement, especially when customers have access to all the information, products, and brands in the world. Despite the advent of the internet, the mere exposure effect can still be used to close sales. Put your name in front of your audience. Introduce yourself, again and again, to potential customers. The more they see your name and product in their everyday life, the more positively they will respond to seeing you again. This positivity and confidence lend themselves to more sales and a higher value for your brand.

How will you know that your customers are seeing your message? Get to know your customers through buyer personas and market research. Where do your customers shop? How much time do they spend online, and what social media sites are most popular? Are they more likely to see ads on the subway or on a billboard next to the highway? On Google or on a Facebook page? Answering all of these questions will give you a better idea of where to put your message.

A handful of different messages will not make as much impact as one sole message that continues to gain trust and favor with your audience. Push a singular message and let the mere exposure effect do the rest of the work. Make your message and design familiar. There is no need to reinvent the wheel, especially when the wheel is loved and trusted by your customers. **Rather than exhaust time and resources looking for a unique website design or style, use a format that is familiar and has stood the test of time.**

Do not directly copy a brand or competitor, but do not feel the need to stray so far away to make yourself stand out. While your message can be unique, the best ways of conveying it have already been tested by others. Other brands before you have already done the work of familiarizing your audience with a specific design or layout. Analyze, measure, repeat.

There is a very fine line between familiarizing your audience with your message and drowning them in it. Too much exposure can have a negative effect on your brand. This line is not crossed overnight, so it's important for your team to stay vigilant and monitor how your audience is responding to advertisements or messages that you are sending out. We've all heard a jingle that was catchy at first but eventually made us grumble and boycott the brand forever out of principle. Do not let your messages or your pitch get to that point. Stay on top of market research to determine how customers are responding to your messages.

In general, it is more common for a new entrepreneur to have too little exposure rather than too much. It is important that you put yourself out there and introduce (or reintroduce) your brand to your audience. Keep mere exposure theory in the back of your mind as you develop your overall marketing strategy.

28

Anchoring Your Price

Picture this. You pull up to a gas station where a gallon of gas is $2.00. As you are waiting in line to pay, you hear a grandmother huffing over the price of gas. She remembers when gas was 10 cents for a gallon, so paying $2.00 is just ridiculous. Behind her is a driver in their mid-20s. When they started driving, gas was at an all-time high. Paying $2.00 for gas is nothing compared to $4.00. Behind this driver is someone from New Zealand; they pay $2.00 for a liter of petrol when they drive, so they feel comfortable with prices, even if they are different units of measurement. Whose opinion is "right?"

All the drivers in line may think the one behind them is over-exaggerating, but every person is "anchored" in their idea of how much a gallon of gas should cost. Telling the grandmother that gas is more expensive now won't necessarily make her feel better about paying $2.00 for gas. The "anchoring effect" can have a big impact on how customers react to prices and sales –even if products are being priced fairly.

The anchoring effect creates a reference point in our minds from the first thing that we see or recognize. We often refer to that anchor as we make decisions or take in the world around us. The number of experiences that we have "anchored" in our mind may not be the same as other people, but because it was our first impression, we continue to go back to it. We can change our frame of reference over time, but when we are in a similar environment, we tend to feel uncomfortable straying from what we view as "normal."

Anchoring doesn't just appear in sales. Our frame of reference is hard to budge, even as we get a new job or move to a new location. The ideas and values instilled in us as we grew up and first experienced the world will have a lasting effect on our expectations. Understanding the anchoring effect can help you get into the mind of your customers and see where they are coming from.

In his book "Influence," Professor Robert Cialdini recounts an episode that occurred at an American airport. At the gate of an overbooked flight, an operator jokingly announced that the airline would offer a $100,000 voucher to the passenger willing to give up their seat. He immediately corrected that sum to $100, causing a laugh among the passenger queuing at the gate. An expensive laugh for the airline because, at that point, the passengers were "anchored" on that high sum, compared to which the $100 looked like a pittance, and nobody took the offer. Wouldn't it have been better to jokingly offer $1 instead?

"Anchors" vary for every person, especially among **different demographics.** Think back to the gas example. The price of gas was wildly different for each person, based on their age and where they were from. Refer to your customer avatar to understand how your prospect will view prices and the world at large.

Remember that, as a professional in your industry, your reference point may be more accurate than your customers, but it's important to step into your customers' shoes for the anchoring effect to work in your favor. **Don't base your strategy on what you think is the right price for your products...base it on your customers' ideas.**

Determine where your customers get their information about pricing in your industry. How do they know what a product like yours would cost? What prices have they been exposed to before? How long have they shopped in your industry?

Discounts should always consider a customer's frame of reference before they are implemented. If $50 for a product is your reference point, a 50% discount on a $50 product will appear to be a steal. A 50% discount on the same item that was originally priced at $100 will not necessarily elicit the same response.

As your customers move throughout the buyer's journey, they are going to see different prices from your business and from your competitors. As you create content for customers along their journey, consider what prices you will include. If your customers are looking for value in their purchase, put higher prices on content for potential customers. Bring prices down once these customers have expressed interest in your brand and made a purchase.

If you are discussing prices directly with a customer, keep the anchoring effect in mind. If you are having trouble coming to a price that you both agree on, acknowledge that you may be coming from two different viewpoints. Finding common ground can help you explain why your products are a good value and how they can benefit your customer.

The best way to sell a $20 pair of jeans is to put it next to a $100 pair of jeans. Anchoring plays a big part in price comparisons, especially when the two prices have a big gap. A study at the University of Arizona created two real estate pamphlets: one featured real estate with fair prices, and the other featured real estate with over-inflated prices. When these two pamphlets were given to participants (including real estate professionals), they were swayed more by the expensive real estate. The cheaper real estate looked like a great value and a steal compared to the over-inflated prices, even though that real estate was priced fairly, to begin with.

Get creative and consider how your prices "anchor" customers one way or the other. Can you persuade your customers that your products are the best value compared to what they think are fair prices?

29

Understanding Pricing Tiers

Initially, pricing your products can be intimidating. What do your customers consider a good price for the value of your products and all their benefits? The answer may be higher or lower than you expect, and you should not miss out when the answer is higher. When you are pricing products, offer pricing tiers (or packages) at multiple prices to secure higher purchases from customers who are willing to spend.

Pricing tiers can rack up more sales, rack up higher sales, and give your customers the opportunity to show you what they are looking for.

Let's start by talking about the advantages of having products with a low price point. Products under $50 are pocket change compared to larger price points with three and four digits. This **smaller price point encourages more impulse buys**. New customers who are just introduced to your product are more likely to grab on impulse a product under $50 if you can catch their attention. Other factors that encourage impulse buys include:

- **Size.** If someone can't walk away carrying the product or throwing it in a bag, they will be less likely to grab it at a moment's notice.)
- **Cross merchandising**. The product is placed next to other products that pair well.

- **Immediate recognition.** If the product grabs the attention and can quickly display how it fits someone's needs.
- **Low risk.** If the purchase is a low risk, not too much deliberation has to go into the purchase.

As you raise the prices, remember that the larger the price point, the larger the wiggle room for the customer. When you reach three-and four-digit prices, consumers tend to deliberate more about their purchases. But the exact price of your product may not make a difference over the value of its benefits and how it fits your customer's needs. The higher your price point, the higher the range of "right" prices. In the above price range, $50 doesn't make too much of a difference from $40. Either price encourages an impulse buy, despite what competitors have priced for similar products.

Customers are less likely to notice changes in price when prices are already so low. In fact, **slashing prices when prices are already low may have a negative effect.** Customers look to get the best value rather than the lowest price. Simply changing a number may not be the best strategy.

As products approach higher price points, this wiggle room gets larger and larger. If customers are looking at products that are priced over $1,500, they may be willing to pay a larger range for products. The difference between a $1,799 product and a $1,900 product may be as minuscule as the difference between a $40 product and a $50 product. *Weber's Law* explains this phenomenon by saying that the change in prices isn't noticeable until it has changed by 10%.

Of course, simply changing a number isn't the only factor that will influence a customer to buy one product over the other. When you compare your prices to competitors, consider factors like brand loyalty, accessibility, and the perceived value of your product.

Different price points give you the potential to close more sales and learn more about what your customers are looking for. If you offer a product at $50, you will only know how many customers are willing to pay $50 for your product. This information may not tell you much about your customers, especially when you consider how this price range encourages impulse buying. If you offer packages that are $50 and $150, you can make more money on $150 packages and learn how many customers are willing to pay $50 and $150 for your products.

If you expand to $50, $150, and $350 packages, you learn even more about customer preferences and find your way to the sweet spot of packaging, pricing, and what your customers are looking for.

Pricing tiers are not new. You've probably come across them when signing up for subscriptions, websites, or anything that offers different "packages." Before you purchased your item or subscription, you probably had a budget in mind that you were willing to spend and saw that price reflected in one of the packages. Packages typically include different groups of products or benefits; as the package increases, so do the price and the value. **High-priced packages do not have to cost your company more money**, however.

Remember that customers consider a product or service "a steal" when there is a high difference between the perceived value and the price. The fulfillment cost of the product or service has no space in these considerations. If you are offered a phone plan for $8 a month, you will consider that a great deal, even though it costs the phone company just a few cents to add your number to the network. Again, it is all about the difference between the price and the perceived value.

Here are some benefits you can include to increase the perceived value of a package without increasing the fulfillment costs for you:

- Warranties or insurance on the purchase.
- Free consultations or trials.

- Exclusive access to deals, pre-sales, etc.
- A longer membership.

When you add different benefits, you learn what your customers are looking for or consider valuable in your product. The first range of pricing tiers that you offer may not be perfect, so continue to experience and test these tiers until you've found a range that works for your customers.

30

Using Sales and Discounts in a Scientific Way

For decades, the most effective sales tactic has been in the name...a sale. Who doesn't want to save money on a product? Cutting prices and offering discounts to customers always seems to grab attention, but is it effective for long-term growth and customer retention?

Scientific research shows that cutting prices can be effective, but only when they are **used as an overall strategy to close sales and express value to customers.**

We will get to the details in a moment. But first, let us clarify what we mean by "Discounting."

There is more to discounting than putting an item on sale. Common discounts include:

- Offering a percentage off items
- Offering free or discounted incentives with each purchase
- Undercutting prices based on competitors
- Offering discounts for purchasing early

· Offering discounts for subscriptions or bundled items

These offers may be made exclusively for customers who sign up for a mailing list or follow a brand's social media accounts. Offers could be made at a certain time of year.

All these offers may have different consequences or effects based on your customer base. Discounts are a great strategy that can be used at all points of the customer journey. An email subject line that offers discounts on free products is more likely to be opened than one simply advertising products. Sales of discounted products can convert new customers into loyal supporters of your brand. Loyal customers often expect, and certainly appreciate, a reward for sticking with a brand and continuing to purchase its products. An incentive like "buy ten coffees get one free" is a form of this type of discount.

At first glance, a discount seems like a quick way to grab customers' attention and give them the incentive to buy. However, there is more psychology behind price cutting than meets the eye. The psychology behind sales and discounts has fascinated researchers for decades.

Basic theories and principles support the idea behind discounts. The **Pleasure Principle**, for example, states that people seek pleasure and avoid pain. If customers are looking to make a purchase, it would be more pleasurable to make the purchase during a sale. There is "pain" in having to pay more for the same item after the sale is over. Avoiding the pain of paying more is enough incentive for many people to buy during a sale.

Strategic discounts don't have to take place over a short period of time. One of the most effective discounts is a very simple tactic. Want to know why all sales end in 9? This "discount" (even if it is only 1 dollar or 1 cent) works. Studies from top universities showed that prices that end in 9 sell more items, even if they are more expensive than other items ending in different digits. When in doubt, end your prices with a 9.

This next idea is more complicated and may not apply to all customer segments. Undercutting your competition may not always work out in your favor. Studies have revealed that customers who compare prices may make assumptions about products based on their price; the most common assumption is that **the higher-priced item is a better value or more effective**. Customers may even be skeptical of discounts, and with more information available to customers than ever, customers have more time and resources to think about why a product is discounted compared to competitors.

Customers also tend to respond negatively to constant changes in discounts and prices. If you want to convert customers into loyal supporters and promoters of your brand, you will need to be consistent with your pricing. Overwhelming changes can be confusing and turn people off when they go back to buy another product. Discounts, sales, and other incentives should be communicated clearly, so everyone is on the same page about pricing and the reasons behind price cuts.

How should you implement discounts without turning customers off? Research shows that there is a fine line between discounts that close sales and discounts that close the door to customers forever. Think carefully before you add discounts to your sales strategy. A key to effective discounting is presenting a discount that is valuable to customers. If you offer different price points, offer a discounted price that gives customers more value than other options (it is sometimes better to pump up the offer for the same price rather than reduce the price). Put your customers in the driver's seat. Customers will feel like they are making a smart decision and getting the most out of their purchase.

Expressing value should always be the goal when you are creating content that advertises or offers a sale. The way you communicate a sale can make a difference in whether it is perceived as a good value or a trick that may not be trustworthy. In most cases, giving customers "tips" about how they can save shows that you are looking out for the customer and you want to give them the best deal.

Offering sales as a "thank you" to customers presents the sale as a reward for loyal customers who have stuck by the brand.

The best way to know how your customers will respond to discounts is to get to know them closely (see the chapter on customer research) and analyze the results of different discounts. Ask yourself the following questions. Will your customers look for a product that is more effective or one that will fit in with their lifestyle and budget? Do they tend to shop around big sales? As your customers move through the buyer's journey, how likely are they to respond to sales and advertisements? At what point are they looking at competitors and their pricing?

Beginner entrepreneurs tend to abuse discounts. They sometimes act as if putting their product on sale will automatically guarantee that people will buy it. It does not work that way at all. Do as much research as you can before offering a discount. If you do end up offering one, carefully analyze the results of the discount. So many factors play into whether customers respond to a discount; it may take a few trials to figure out exactly what type is most effective for your business.

Discounts that are given without proper strategy may succeed but will only promote growth if they are added, implemented, and measured along with your overall sales strategy.

31

Building Trust in Your Customers

Who would you rather take out a loan from a woman in a 3-piece suit or a woman in sweatpants? Let's rephrase the question. Who would you rather take out a loan from a woman in a 3-piece suit whom you have never met before or a woman in sweatpants whom you have done business with for over ten years without any issues?

We trust the first woman in the first example because she is wearing the right clothes to give out a loan. We trust the second woman in the second example because we have been loyal business partners with her and have had no issues.

This chapter isn't about whether you should wear sweatpants to work. It's about building trust with your customers. Without customer trust, you won't have any customers.

Salespeople have a hard job here. When you first enter the world of business with your product or service to offer, you will have to face the harsh reality that many customers are wary of talking to sales representatives just because of what they do. No one wants to be swindled into making a bad purchase. Luckily, an open and honest dialogue about the customer and their needs will help you build trust in every interaction.

Keep the following tips in mind when you create content or speak to customers throughout their journey:

Understand their needs. A customer who is curious about your products or brand but not looking to buy is probably not going to respond well to a hard pitch. Understand where your customer is at on the buyer's journey. This understanding can initially be communicated through a cold advertisement, cold calling, or other types of marketing that bring a customer to your website. In order to get a customer interested in your company or product, it is necessary that you give them a solution that they are looking for.

Ask and listen. The best way to find the information you are looking for is to ask and listen. What brought them to your website or to your office? What similar products do they own now, and what are their thoughts on those products? What questions do they have about your products or brands? When they answer, listen. If you meet your customer at their particular point on the journey, you are more likely to guide them further to being a customer and active supporter of your brand.

Use testimonials and social proof. We talked about both techniques in earlier chapters. Social proof and testimonials from customers help establish trust by showing them how your business and products have worked for similar people. Credibility and trust go hand in hand. Have testimonials and awards available at your desk to pull out during a sales interaction.

Look at your sale from a customer-centric approach. Inbound marketing, social media, and smartphones have rapidly changed the way customers are approached and treated by businesses. Customers are beginning to expect a sales pitch that appeals directly to their needs. Once you've gathered their needs, find them a solution. The solution may or may not involve your products or your business yet, but doing them a favor with an answer is bound to establish trust and satisfy the customer.

Offer free value. Want to show your customer that you care about them? Give them something for free. Whether you offer a free sample, consultation, or trial run of your product, a free trial draws customers in and builds trust. Who can say no to free stuff, anyway?

Be truthful, even when it's not positive. Skeptical buyers are always asking themselves one question: "What's the catch?" They are looking for a reason not to trust you or your products. If you present them with any negatives truthfully and openly, it's less likely to come across as a "catch." If you try and hide any downsides or negative answers, the customer will feel as though they caught you in a "gotcha!" moment, and you will lose their trust. Highlight your strengths but be willing to admit and own up to shortcomings.

Be consistent. We have already tackled this aspect in a previous chapter. If you are consistent with your message and your top values, you will build trust with your customers faster. All customers want to hear is the truth to make a well-informed decision. Stick to a consistent truth throughout your relationship with each customer, and they will come to expect the truth.

What if you lost the customer's trust? Can you rebuild it? Not all sales go the way that you want them to. Not all businesses or companies are as honest as they should be. A PR scandal or a faulty product can seem like the end of the world for salespeople who want to keep their customers coming back. Luckily, there are ways to rebuild trust after losing customers.

Get feedback. Like objection handling, losing a customer can still be a positive experience if you get proper feedback and learn how to grow and change moving forward. Continue to ask questions about where your business missed the mark and what expectations were not met. Asking and listening show the customer that you care about their needs and aren't just waiting to make your next pitch. (Or that you're waiting very, very patiently.)

Find common ground. Even if you are not seeing eye-to-eye with someone, you can find common ground. Empathize with disappointed customers and let them vent their frustrations. Once a customer knows that you are on their side, they are more likely to trust you again.

Be patient. Trust is not an easy thing to rebuild. If you find yourself getting frustrated or irritated, step away from the interaction. Negative emotions or rushed pitches will come off as desperate, and any trust that you've built up will be unraveled again.

Rebuilding trust is an even longer process than building trust, so be patient. One or two interactions may not seem like they are making a difference, but consistently showing your customers that you care will help to build a stronger customer relationship than ever before.

If you are at the beginning of your entrepreneurial journey, don't stress about building trust just yet (but also don't expect everyone you meet to hand over their cash immediately).

Be patient, consistent, and empathetic to your customers, and you will build a solid level of trust.

32

Priming Your Customers

By now, you have probably heard this phrase: "It's not what you say. It's how you say it." One technique that allows us to send a message more effectively is priming. Priming should be at the forefront of your mind before every conversation, email, sales call, and in general, when you approach your marketing, as it influences how customers think throughout the buyer's journey.

Priming is a technique that trains our mind to respond to stimuli based on how we were exposed to those stimuli in the past. What we initially see or hear will continue to influence our thinking. Priming is not always done intentionally but can be used in sales and marketing to train customers to believe or respond to different messages or products.

There are many ways in which we are primed to "fill in the blanks" or think a certain way due to past stimuli or memories. Let's look at a few examples to see how easily priming can adjust our thinking.

Who Is Who? Below are three sentences that either describes an "angel" or a "devil." Assign the role to one of the options. Do not think too hard about the answer.

Option 1: They are generous and kind. They live a life that they enjoy. They know how to get what they want, no matter what it takes.

Option 2: They know how to get what they want, no matter what it takes. They live a life that they enjoy. They are generous and kind.

Before you finished reading the description of Option 1, you may have guessed that this was describing the "angel." By the time you finished Option 2, you may have noticed that both options contain the same content. Our first impressions shape our opinions, even if we have not gotten the full picture. This is a result of strategic priming.

Filling in the Blank. Let's look at another example. Fill in the blanks below:
   S_ _ _ S
   P _ _ _ _ _ G

Did you answer "sales" and "priming?" Those words could be anything: stems, picking, sends, padding. "Sales" and "priming" are at the forefront of our minds, so we naturally pick those words first.

Professors vs. "Soccer hooligans." Priming was brought into mainstream discussions after it was mentioned in Malcolm Gladwell's 2005 book *Blink: The Power of Thinking Without Thinking.* The book mentions an experiment conducted by Dutch researchers. The researchers took two groups of people who were about to play Trivial Pursuit. One group was asked to think about being a professor for some time prior to the game. Another group was asked to think about being a "soccer hooligan." The groups were pitted against each other in Trivial Pursuit, and who do you think won? The group that thought about being a professor. This group was no smarter than the other group, but they had been "primed" to play Trivial Pursuit by thinking about someone who is revered as intelligent. Starting the game with this frame of mind primed them to play smarter.

How can you use priming to make your marketing more effective and boost your sales?

Gladwell's experiment speaks to just one of the ways that priming can be applied to sales. Whether you are introducing yourself to potential buyers online or having a final meeting to discuss final purchases, you can prime your customers in a way that will leave them positive and confident in their purchase. Much of intentional priming requires us to rearrange our conversations and interactions so that we begin with words, images, or other stimuli that lead to our end goal: closing the sale.

We have already discussed the importance of market research, which means getting to know your potential customers in detail. Why are they coming to you in the first place? What are their top priorities: price, durability, safety? What about their demographics or lifestyle leads them to value certain features over others? Once you know what buyers are looking for and why they are looking for it, you can begin to construct a message that gets their attention. If you are selling a car to mothers who are looking for a safe car for their family, you know that mentioning safety for children will get their attention. By priming your message and mentioning child safety features first, you will immediately send the message that your car is one that will fit your buyers' needs. If you lead with information that is irrelevant, like the look of the car or the price, they will be turned off before you can mention safety or more desirable features. To create an effective message through priming, you will have **to collect the messages that you want to communicate with customers and make sure to present them first** (keep in mind the Who Is Who example). Priming allows customers to hear and internalize your messages within seconds.

Let's reflect on the experiment mentioned in Gladwell's book. At some point before playing Trivial Pursuit, each group was primed, and their performance was set in stone. The buyer's journey can be a long game to play. Potential buyers may visit a company's website or visit a store multiple times before making a purchase. Think of this time as the time participants were given to think about being a professor or a "soccer hooligan." *What mindset are you putting your customers in?* Are they thinking about buying your products?

Seeing an image or reading stories from similar buyers who made a purchase with you will get customers in the purchasing mindset, even if they are not ready to close the sale. Keep your end goals in mind as you guide your buyers along on their journey and try to prime them to close the sale.

Lead with Positivity. Priming can also be applied to direct sales and customer service. If you want your customers to have a good experience, lead with positive messages and experiences. Even if they are hesitant to listen to your pitch or buy that day, a positive message will lift their spirits. Start your email with a comment on the local sports team that is doing well or a genuine compliment. Conversely, answering the phone in a gruff tone or complaining about the weather will immediately put a bad taste in a buyer's mouth. Create an environment of trust and comfort, so your customers are willing to open up and listen to your sales pitch. Priming can be used on a grand scale but can also be applied to a single sentence. If you are breaking some bad news to a customer, squeeze in a hopeful note to begin. Lead with good news or benefits of your product before discussing setbacks or concerns.

Remember that priming has a huge impact on how we sell and communicate. Keep these ideas in mind as you sell, and continue to check in and ask how you are "priming" your customers to close sales. What initial words, images, or stimuli are you using to influence your customers? How will your first impression have an impact on the rest of your interaction? Are your priming techniques appropriate for your buyers? Let your customers fill in the blanks and trust in your business through priming.

33

Reciprocity in Marketing

As we go through our day, people may do good deeds for us. As we accept the deed or the gift, we may automatically feel the urge to return the deed or do something positive as well. If someone invites you to a holiday party, you are more likely to keep them in mind when you are making the guest list for the next party you host. When someone offers to pay for a round of drinks at the bar, you may want to pick up the next round. You may be more obliged to pick up a flier from someone on the street that gives you a compliment.

Even if we do not previously know the person who committed the good deed, we may feel a positive connection and be compelled to help them in the future. This is the power of the rule of reciprocity: it stirs up these feelings of wanting to do a good deed and can be used by brands and salespeople to get favorable results from customers.

Robert Cialdini explains the "rule of reciprocation" as one of his six rules of influence. This rule states that when humans receive a gift or act of kindness, they want to return the favor. The favor may not be immediately returned, and it may not be returned in the same form as the original good deed. A person may return the favor in a day, a year, or never, but the original good deed will most likely be remembered and build trust between the giver and the receiver.

When Cialdini studied the rule of reciprocity, he looked at the Hare Krishna movement. You may have seen members of this movement moving through cities, singing songs, dancing, and giving away gifts to strangers. This last tactic isn't just a pastime for hippies; it's a recruitment tactic that works. Cialdini observed the movement raise millions of dollars through these little gifts.

As a small business owner, you can use the rule of reciprocity by creating and offering content, discounts, or other "gifts" throughout the buyer's journey. Gifts that invoke the reciprocity principle do not have to cost your business a lot of money but can yield a high return and move potential customers closer to being active supporters and promoters of your brand.

Let's start with the first introduction of your brand. Customers may visit your website through a blog post, Internet search, or referral. An informative blog post can already be a good deed for potential customers; readers who come across a blog post are usually looking for the answer to questions or further information about a problem or need. If your brand has that information at hand, you are already fulfilling your customers' needs. To keep them coming back to your website and add them to your mailing list, you may want to offer a gift first, such as:

- A free eBook with information relevant to their needs.
- A discount on their first purchase.

If you advertise your mailing list as a gift (free information, exclusive offers, etc.), potential customers will be more willing to add their names to the mailing list. Once a potential customer has signed up for a mailing list, you can offer additional gifts or favors that are more appropriate to customers that have shown interest in your brand.

Studies show that 70% of customers open an advertising email with the hope of finding a gift or discount. The rule of reciprocity plays a big part in content marketing: when you continue to provide accurate and informative answers to potential customers who have questions, they will have a positive reaction and trust your brand.

Treat informative content as a way to help your audience. Customers who have tried or purchased your product hold the ability to review and promote your product. When you ship or deliver a product to your customers, including extra gifts or discounts along with a feedback form will give customers more encouragement to write a testimonial or share their experiences on social media. Again, research shows that 39% of customers are more likely to give a positive referral after receiving an incentive to do so.

Brands can also offer good deeds, product samples, or discount codes after purchase to further the relationship. Having these extra gifts encourages one-time customers to become loyal supporters or active promoters of your brand.

You must perfect your strategy in offering free gifts and incentives. Offering a discount to someone who has never heard of your company may not be as effective as offering a discount to a customer who is just about to make a decision to buy your product. Before you offer gifts with monetary value to customers, run a sample test stop to see if your audience will use or remember what they received.

Keep in mind that the reciprocity rule doesn't have to yield instant results. You will be playing a long-term game.

Implement reciprocity in all aspects of your business. Every interaction with your customer is an opportunity to offer a kind deed or favor that could eventually result in a positive interaction that works in your favor. Offering a coffee at your desk or even the offer to call your customers back at a time when they aren't busy could go a long way.

There is a caveat to all this. People are less likely to react positively if they feel as though a gift has ulterior motives behind it. **When you are offering a gift or doing a good deed for your customers, do so to benefit them, not you**. Be genuine, and do not expect an immediate return for your good deed.

Remember that there is a difference between offering a favor and offering a favor in return for a favor. If you continue to bait potential customers around with incentives, they will eventually lose interest and turn to a brand that is offering gifts or favors without any strings attached.

34

Implementing Scarcity

If you just walked out of a restaurant and you are full of food and drinks, stopping next door for a $50 burger may not sound appealing at all. If you haven't had a meal in days, that $50 burger may sound like the best offer you've ever heard. Nothing has changed about the burger or its price; your need for food has affected your decision-making skills and the appeal of an overpriced burger.

Let's look at another example. You are choosing flowers to pick for your garden. An advertisement for one type of flower boasts that this flower grows all over the world and is rather popular in your area. Another flower is extremely rare, and the flower that you buy may, in fact, be the last generation of this flower before it disappears forever. They are the same price, but for some reason, the rare flower becomes a lot more appealing than one that you can get any day of the week. This is the power of the scarcity mindset at work.

Scarcity is another psychological principle popularized by Robert Cialdini in his book *Influence*. Cialdini explains that when humans think that they are running out of a particular product, purchasing it becomes more appealing. We can relate it to the simple economic concept of supply and demand: low supply leads to high demand.

Scarcity influences how we make decisions beyond purchases. The scarcity mindset influences how we conduct business, how we relate to other people, and even how we date. The opposite of a scarcity mindset (the "abundance" mindset) has become a goal for many business leaders to create an environment with positivity and control. A scarcity mindset can take over our decisions and leaves many people feeling out of control, even when they have an abundance of wealth, time, or other resources.

Why do Americans spend $80 billion on cigarettes each year? The lack of nicotine in their bodies directs them to keep buying. Even in states that heavily tax cigarettes, addicted smokers move their budgets around to satisfy their needs when they are scarce. Scarcity can directly relate to our physical needs, but a scarcity of something can be created in our minds.

Have you, or anyone you know, bought a new car during a "midlife crisis?" The scarcity mindset goes deeper than just hunger in this scenario. When a person begins to think that there is a small amount of time left, a fancy car or a new house becomes even more appealing. With "no time left," the customer is urged to buy now. There is no physical need to satisfy when you are buying the last hand soap on the counter, but scarcity works in this way too. When there are only one or two items left, we are more tempted to purchase them. After all, seeing a sole product on display is a sign that the product is running out. People like it, and we better seize the last opportunity not to miss out on it.

The scarcity mindset plays a large factor in the purchase decisions of people throughout different economic classes. But there is no need to terrorize your potential customers. There are many ways to use the scarcity principle to subtly influence purchase decisions without doom and gloom. Even a simple word or phrase can boost the value of a product by framing it as scarce in supply.

Once again, market research is fundamental to properly executing tactics that will appeal to your customers' needs. One key element of the scarcity mindset is an intense focus on satisfying needs. A hungry person may not even spend $1 on anything else if it means they have $1 less to buy food. As you get to know your customers, ask yourself the following questions: What are they spending their money on currently? What are they saving up for? If they buy your product, what are they sacrificing (if they are sacrificing anything?)

Structuring your content and pitching to customers' needs will make your products seem more appealing. Of course, scarcity in sales isn't always so complex. Have you ever booked a flight and read that there are only "2 seats left at this price!" Or, shopped online and read that "This offer ends today." Scarcity also works if you convince customers that a great value, or a product itself, is running out. Scarce supply increases its value. Customers will think of the disappointment or pain that they may feel if they miss out on a great deal and make a faster decision to buy the product.

Companies use the terms "exclusive" or "limited edition" to invoke the scarcity mindset and convince customers to grab the item before it's gone forever. Consider how you are urging your customers to make a purchase decision. Ask yourself the following questions on how scarcity plays into your sales tactics: Will the available time and supply influence create extra value? How can you express this value? Is your product something that will benefit your customers now or in the future? How can your product satisfy current needs that are at the forefront of your customer's minds?

The answers to all these questions can help boost the appeal of your products and urge customers to make a purchase decision sooner rather than later. Creating a scarcity mindset can have a huge impact on purchase decisions and might close a sale sooner than you think.

35

The Similarity-Attraction Principle

Many factors play into a purchase decision, including the product's value and the person behind the product.

To sell a product, you must sell yourself and make yourself a likable person. Your personality may not affect how the product actually works or how it will benefit the customer, but it will certainly have an effect on whether or not a customer wants to go through with the purchase. No one wants to buy a product from a brand or a salesperson that they do not like.

There are many qualities that make a person likable, but in this chapter, we will specifically look at how similarity attracts people. If customers find that they are similar to you or similar to the people who work for your business, they are more likely to be attracted to you and follow through with a sale.

What is the Similarity-Attraction Principle? Simply put, people are attracted to other people who are similar to them. Similarities could include interests, demographics, backgrounds, attitudes, etc. The more you have in common with another person, the more likely you are to be attracted to them and want to be around them. The similarity-attraction works in a similar way to the mere exposure effect discussed earlier in the book. Two people who live in the same area are more likely to be exposed to the same stimuli and are more likely to be familiar with and attracted to each other.

Research studying the similarity-attraction principle was popularized in the 1960s. Studies have looked at a variety of similarities, from height in romantic couples to attitudes and beliefs in roommates and friend groups. Not every similarity between two people results in an immediate attraction. People with similar morals or values, for example, are more likely to be attracted to each other than people who are fans of the same sports team.

You do not have to force yourself to watch the same television shows as your customers to sell products but finding common ground in your values and attitude certainly helps. If you have a larger customer base, this idea can be overwhelming. How can you find (and keep track of) similar interests with everyone that you interact? How can your content bring in clients? Is adding a movie reference or information about your hobbies isolating?

In general, your customer base will lead the conversation on how to create relatable and likable content. Follow your customers' lead, and you will find yourself in a more comfortable conversation.

Once again, market research is the starting point. Look for common ground among your entire customer base. They already have one thing in common (interest in your product.) Go deeper than demographics to look for values. What jobs do they hold? What type of homes do they live in? What are their long-term goals? Do your customers want to buy a product that is safe for their families? Do they want to use their product to better themselves? What values or beliefs have led them to their current position? You may be able to find these answers through market research or customer surveys.

Finding common ground with your client base doesn't have to involve research if you are a locally-based business. If you service exclusively local clientele, you can find common ground by attending local events and getting involved in the community. Include regional dialect in your content and include information about how long you have been working in the area. Getting yourself into the community outside of advertisements shows customers that you take pride in your home, a similarity that goes deeper than other interests or attitudes.

The same principle applies to current trends on social media or in the local area. An in-depth knowledge of hashtags, memes, or fads shows that you speak your customers' language. Do not be afraid to be more colloquial on social media, especially if you are trying to appeal to a younger customer base or want to showcase a more fun and quirkier brand. Remember to be genuine as you are trying to "stay hip." Sharing a meme that doesn't make sense will come off as a strange marketing gimmick that doesn't create brand trust or likability.

Add personality and likability to your landing page. Landing pages are a great place to include information about yourself or your business that customers can relate to. Do not be afraid to list your favorite sports teams or hobbies in your biography on your website, as well as the core values that you want to bring to each sale and each interaction. Customers who have similar interests will remember these facts and may bring them up in emails or conversations. The more information you include about your interests and background, the more likely a similar person will catch on and want to know more.

Get to know individual customers. If you are working with individual customers over time, incorporating the similarity-attraction principle may be easier. Do not be afraid to spend time talking to your customers about the game that was on last week or the latest movie that came out. Stay away from political topics or other controversial discussions that could cause tension if you disagree. Ask questions about your customers to learn more about their interests and how you can relate to them.

Perform excellent customer service. Keep the similarity-attraction principle in mind as you provide high-quality customer service. If your customers hold the belief that "the customer is always right," they will hold you to a high standard and expect you to cater to their needs to make the sale. Conduct each interaction with positivity and likability. Open up to your customers to find common ground that you can connect on throughout your interactions.

Finding similarities and striving for likability does not have to be complicated. Follow the values held by your customers and see where your brand or personality genuinely intersects. Showcase your similarities, and you will continue to build trust and confidence in every interaction.

36

Social Proof

Say you're in a completely new city with no clue where to go for dinner. Often, people have three options in this scenario. The first is looking online for highly rated restaurants in the city. Websites like TripAdvisor or Yelp make finding a decent restaurant a breeze; past diners share their experiences and give you the best idea of what to expect at the restaurant.

The second option is to go to the hotel lobby and ask the concierge for their recommendations. Hotels usually have a list of events, sights, and restaurants that guests will enjoy in the area. The person at the desk may also have some personal recommendations; after all, they live nearby.

The third option is to wander throughout the city and look for restaurants. In this case, pretend you are looking at two different diners on the same street. One is alive with many guests and even a wait out the door. The other is completely empty. Which one do you think will give you the better meal? These three options may seem like different ways to find a good restaurant, but they are, in fact, all examples of social proof in action.

Social proof is a great way to establish credibility with new customers who are otherwise unfamiliar with your business.

Robert Cialdini brought the Social Proof Theory into light in 1984. He said that when humans are looking for correct behavior, they will look towards other humans for an example. Often, they imitate the people around them and trust that they are doing the correct thing. The social proof theory could be applied to many behaviors. For example, if you are in a new country and do not know the proper dining etiquette, you may look around to see how everyone else is eating. You may not know the intricacies of how to dine, but you know that you are not horribly missing the mark if you eat like everyone else around you.

The same idea goes for purchasing decisions. We may not know why there is a huge line at one restaurant, but we are confident standing in line with everyone else rather than going into a restaurant that is unoccupied.

There are six different types of social proof that you may see in an advertisement, on a website, or just walking down the street:

Expert: If the top fashion blogger in the country thinks that one brand of jeans is the best, their followers and subscribers are going to start buying those jeans. Quoting an expert is a popular form of social proof; after all, they are an expert and know the industry very well.

Celebrity: Your celebrity crush drinks Pepsi? Your daughter's favorite singer shops at H&M? Your favorite athlete uses Tide Pods? Having a celebrity endorsement on your side is a huge win for your company, especially if the endorsement is done naturally through social media or paparazzi photos.

User: TripAdvisor and Yelp are so popular because you read actual reviews from real users about sights, tours, or restaurants. Real users speak your language, and their review sounds like advice rather than an advertisement.

"Wisdom of the Crowds:" Have you ever heard of FOMO (the "Fear of Missing Out?")? If everyone is rushing to buy the newest fad, most likely, we will eventually follow suit. Social Proof Theory tells us that we can't be the only ones without a specific gadget or hottest label.

"Wisdom of Your Friends:" Let's go back to the restaurant example. If your best friend had given you a restaurant recommendation, you probably wouldn't be in the predicament above because your mind would already be made up. We trust our friends and inner circle before we trust anyone else; their recommendation is often worth more than celebrity endorsements or testimonials from strangers.

Certification: A certification, badge, or award is proof that a third party recognizes your achievements or value. Let's go back to the example from earlier. If someone is walking by two empty restaurants and see a certification from TripAdvisor on one, they will more likely choose that restaurant over the other. Even if the certification recognizes the restaurant as "good" rather than "the best," you can have confidence that at least someone has had a good experience at the restaurant.

Keeping the Social Proof Theory in mind, the following tactics can help direct potential customers to your business and give them the confidence that they, and everyone around them, can be confident in their purchase.

Testimonials: Add testimonials to your content. If a customer sees people are happy with your brand and happy with their purchase, they will have the confidence to think that they will be happy with you too. Studies show that if you add photos of customers to your testimonials, they will be more effective since they appear more real. Want to get more testimonials or reviews of your brand? Ask! Send out surveys and feedback requests to customers on your mailing list. Add incentives (discounts, the potential of sharing the review on social media, etc.) to get more feedback.

Displaying your Certifications and Badges: Displaying awards and achievements in your office isn't bragging. It's building trust with your customers.

Whether you or your product has earned an award, the extra validation adds value to the product that you are trying to sell.

Stats: How many cars in this model were sold last year? What was the bestselling product on the market? How many people invested in this company? Having stats on hand can show customers how many people have already bought into your brand. Stats are a way of showing a restaurant line out the door. When a customer sees how many other people believe buying your brand is appropriate behavior, Social Proof Theory will kick in, and they will also believe that they are doing the right thing by purchasing with you.

Understanding Social Proof Theory allows potential customers to build trust in your business based on what other people are saying. Beef up your content with positive reviews and certifications to bring people in and entice them to learn more about your business.

37

Creating Effective Testimonials

It's no secret that testimonials provide major benefits to businesses and products throughout all industries. Studies have reported that 90%of participants who read positive online reviews said that they were influenced by them. At any stage of the buyer's journey, testimonials can be shared to build trust, generate leads, and close sales. B2Band B2C businesses across all industries find **testimonials are one of the top content marketing methods**.

With so many ways to produce and share content, businesses can get extra creative with testimonials. Whether you create an entire landing page dedicated to testimonials or simply share reviews one by one on your Facebook page, this type of content can boost your ROI and create a great buzz about your products.

Before we talk about how to create an effective testimonial, let's discuss why testimonials are effective in the first place. We've talked about similar effects in previous chapters. If potential customers see other people raving about, or even using, a product, they are more inclined to use that product. In the chapter about Social Proof, we discussed the popularity of websites like TripAdvisor or Yelp. People all over the world read a stranger's review of a restaurant or tour and often solely use those reviews while making a purchase decision.

Even though your customers may not know the faces behind the testimonial, they will still take it into consideration. Research has shown that 88% of people still trust a stranger's testimonials. Testimonials have the power to tell a story separate from a sales pitch. Customers who have strong emotions toward your brand or product can reach an audience that may be unsure or unconvinced. A good story is more effective than rattling off facts or statistics about your products. On a less emotional note, using testimonials in content marketing costs less than other traditional marketing methods. All your team has to do is collect testimonials, edit the content, and strategically share the testimonial with your audience. Unless you are using monetary incentives to collect testimonials, this highly effective form of marketing won't cost you a single dime! Positive reviews are very beneficial; failing to use them on your social media pages or on website copy is missing out on a large opportunity.

Testimonials are often cheap and easy to produce but will not always result in higher sales or deeper trust with your customers. The *placement, content,* and *intentions* behind your testimonials all factor into whether they will influence your customers to move along the buyer's journey.

Why Is the Product Great? An effective testimonial doesn't just tell customers that your products are great. A great product for one person is not necessarily a great product for someone else. To write an effective testimonial, customers have to describe why the product has been so great for them. What are the benefits of using the product? How has the product helped this person in their life, and how long have they or been using it? Don't forget to include personal information about the customers that are giving the testimonial. Include a name, age, photo, or any demographic information that may be relevant to your audience.

If you are trying to sell to teachers, including information about the customer as a teacher. If you are trying to expand to a different district or county, share testimonials from residents of that area and include that information in the testimonial. This small bit of information has the potential to show how similar these customers are to the ones reading the testimonial.

Record Video Testimonials. Bring the message home (and see a higher ROI) by creating and recording a video testimonial to share with your audience. 65% of customers are visual learners, and visual content is 40 times more likely to be shared throughout your customers' social media networks. Including a photo or video with your testimonial is more likely to be seen by not only your customers but also other people in your customers' networks.

Recording a video testimonial gives you control over what the testimonial says. Before you record, let the customer know what type of testimonial you are looking for (i.e., how the customer should introduce themselves, why the products are great, why they keep coming back to your business, etc.) Let the customer talk but be sure to edit the video afterward to keep the testimonial brief and concise.

Be Genuine, not "Sales-y." We have all seen commercials with "customers" who we all know are just paid actors. Your customers can see through fake testimonials. Studies show that 90% of people are less likely to trust a testimonial if it's paired next to "sales-y" or marketing messages. Testimonials are most effective when they are genuinely given by another customer that is relatable and raving about the product because they just want to share how much they enjoy it.

Offer Incentives. Having trouble finding customers who want to write a review? Offer incentives through your mailing list, social media pages, or with every purchase. These incentives don't have to cost you money: even an offer to share reviews on your social media pages will yield more results than simply asking for reviews without any incentive. Free gifts, discounts, or any opportunity for customers to be showcased by the company also make great incentives. Remember the rule of reciprocity; if you do a good deed for your customers, they will be more likely to do a good deed for you (and write a stellar testimonial.)

Add Testimonials Throughout your Website Copy. A concise testimonial is an encouragement to move forward through the buyer's journey. If you place a testimonial next to a call-to-action button on your website (i.e., "Learn More," "Call Now," "Get Your Free Trial Today"), you may be giving customers the final boost they need to take the next step.

38

The Paradox of Choice

Picture yourself at your local grocery store. You are looking to purchase a tub of protein powder without much prior knowledge as to what brands, ingredients, or benefits you are looking for. There is only one brand of protein powder available. The choice has been made for you, but do you feel confident that this brand or mix of ingredients is best for your needs?

Now picture yourself at the grocery store with the same dilemma. The grocery store has three different types of protein powder available. You may make your choice in a few minutes and feel satisfied that after weighing the benefits of each product, you made the decision that is best for you.

Picture yourself once again at the grocery store with the same dilemma, but you have the choice of 30 different protein powders. How long would it take you to make a satisfying choice with so many choices? Hours? Days? Could you confidently choose the best product for your needs in a single trip? These three situations present us with the paradox of choice.

In the first scenario, you did not get to make a choice about which product to buy. You may not be as confident in your purchase. After all, with so many other protein powders on the market, you may not have been able to pick the best one. Conversely, having too many choices can be overwhelming. Thirty protein powders? You may not feel confident in this choice, either! The sweet spot is in the middle, with three (or any reasonable number) choices to pick from. Each product or brand has different benefits or drawbacks that you can assess easily.

Barry Schwartz talks about the Paradox of Choice in his 2004 book of the same name. In Chapter 5, he states his thesis by saying: *"Autonomy and Freedom of choice are critical to our well-being, and choice is critical to freedom and autonomy. Nonetheless, though modern Americans have more choice than any group of people ever has before, and thus, presumably, more freedom and autonomy, we don't seem to be benefiting from it psychologically."*

By reducing choices, brands can reduce the chance that they will overwhelm their customers. Offering a multitude of choices will lead to anxiety and a negative experience for the customer. Advanced technology, e-commerce, and social media present customers with more choices than ever before. Products show up in their inbox, in advertisements, and in front of them every day. Piling on a dozen or more products in a showroom or at a meeting will only heighten anxiety. You want to make your customers comfortable and give them a positive experience. **Keep choices simple.**

You can use this information to instill confidence in your customers. Any number of products could suit your customer's needs, but too many choices could overwhelm them. Take the following steps to make sure you are presenting the best options to your customers to close the sale and leave them feeling confident in their purchase.

Assess your customer's needs. If you are selling in person or have a brick-and-mortar business, ask open-ended questions to narrow your customer's options down. What are they looking for in a product? What are their top priorities? What similar products have they used before, and why did they like/dislike those products? What brings them to you today? Use these answers to narrow down their choices.

This can be done on an individual basis or generalized to different buyer personas or customer types. Even if you are selling online through a website, you can implement this tactic. Ask yourself which products fit certain demographics and why? Offer 2-3 products that best suit their needs. When you present limited choices to your customers, you give them less to deliberate. More focus can be given to each individual product and why they suit their needs.

Suggest additional products when appropriate. Your customer may object to your suggestions. Luckily, you have more choices for them! But before you suggest any other products, ask more open-ended questions. What do your customers like about the choices you've presented them with? What additional features or options would they prefer? How would the products you suggested affect their company, and what other solutions are they looking for? Ease your customers into your product range by suggesting the products that best suit their needs. As they continue to show interest and communicate with you about what they are looking for, open up your range to them. Guide them through this process to help them make a choice that they are confident in.

39

The AIDA Method

Is there a perfect recipe for bringing someone through the buyer's journey? Four stages sound almost too simple to be true, but the AIDA method has been credited as a top recipe for closing sales. This model has stood the test of time for over seven decades and massive changes to the ways that people consume and buy products. Without the four stages of AIDA, potential customers will fall off the buyer's journey.

Pay equal attention to all four letters to see a customer make their way through the initial introduction up to the final closed sale.

A: Awareness. The first stage of selling is building awareness. Your audience cannot make a purchase decision without knowing about your brand and what you offer. The shift of marketing strategies from an outbound to an inbound approach has changed the way that businesses approach this stage. Potential customers commonly become aware of brands through:

- Cold ads (or any type of paid or free advertisements).
- Social media posts.
- Word of mouth.
- Blog posts.

One of the top challenges in the awareness stage is placing our content where our audience will see it. Content marketing strategies focus heavily on overcoming these challenges and making sure that they're seen in a positive manner. Market research and buyer personas are great ways to figure out where customers are looking for solutions and where they are looking for products to buy. Another challenge is making sure the audience sees, pays attention to, and remembers the content.

Even though we have all the information in the world at our fingertips, humans only have a short attention span and can take in a very limited amount of information at one time. If we have one task at hand, we may shut our attention off to everything else. So how do you stand out when so much content is being thrown at your customers every second?

Shock Factor. A SpaceX launch certainly tears people away from any other news, even if just for a few moments. Small distractions may not tear us away from the task at hand, so many advertisers will use a shock factor to break a reader's concentration and pull them into the ad.

Providing Solutions. Blog posts are a top tactic for content marketers because they bring customers straight to a brand's website. When someone is searching for answers on Google, a blog post will give them what they want and potentially give them the name of a product or brand that has the solution ready for them. Once someone has read the blog post, they are only one click away from the brand's homepage or shop.

Let's look at an example. A men's clothing brand has a blog post called "How to Tie A Tie." A potential customer who searches "how to tie a tie" may see the title of the blog post and click on it. After they read the blog post, they are already on the business's website and are more likely to see the brand name or click around the site.

I: Interest. Shocking and informative content have one thing in common:

they are interesting. Once you've gotten someone's awareness, you have your name in their mind by appealing to their interests. Awareness doesn't close a sale; interest moves them along the buyer's journey until the reader is a potential lead or customer.

How can you keep readers interested after your first introduction?

Targeted Advertisements. Let's go back to the blog post example. The men's clothing brand sees that someone has read "How to Tie a Tie." They send out targeted advertisements to those readers. In the next few days, the readers will see Facebook ads that offer an eBook on 50 different methods for tying a tie. To get the eBook, the readers have to give the brand their email address. Offering this next step keeps the brand in the customer's mind and adds a new subscriber to the brand's email list.

More Informative Content. Again, a single introduction will not close every sale. Most customers engage with a handful of content before they take the step to talk to a sales representative or buy a product. Continue to produce and distribute blog posts, eBooks, white papers, etc., that keep your customer engaged and provide them with all the answers that they need.

Teaching them something new will establish you or your brand as an authority and build trust throughout the customer journey.

Free Products. One word is almost guaranteed to tear readers away from what they are doing: FREE. Offering free samples or trials of your product gives readers a reason to know more about you and see what you are all about. Free products also build trust; if they can try the product out for themselves, they can make a more informed decision on whether they want to purchase the product later.

Knowing Your Customers. We keep repeating this point because it is truly crucial. Creating buyer personas is fundamental to knowing what your customers are interested in and understanding what type of content they want to consume. Get to know your customers, where they work, where they live, and what kind of problems they have that you can solve.

D: Desire (or Decision). People buy with their emotions. In addition to playing to interests, you have to play to someone's desires in order to help them make a decision. Like interest, knowing what your audience desires takes market research and careful attention to past customers. Adding emotion to your sales materials will only work if you are playing with the right emotions. Use the following tactics to speak to your readers' emotions.

Email Marketing. Let's go back to the tie example. Once you have their email, you can start to send content that plays to the reader's desires. Why would they want to buy a tie or any article of men's clothing? Are they trying to get a promotion at work? Do they want to impress someone on a date? Do they want to give off the impression that they have money or power? Play to these desires in your email subject line: "Want to learn a party trick? Here's the best way to tie the Kelvin knot." "This tie will have heads turning...so don't wear it around the office." The desire stage is important; it drums up emotions and makes people want your product.

Customer Testimonials. Lock down the desire by talking to past customers and paint a picture for future customers. Reach out to past customers who fit the demographic you are trying to reach. Ask them how the product got their attention. Make sure to write down exactly what they say, and then use that when selling your product.

A: Action. You've drummed up desire, but your customers may not take action until you take action. Asking the big questions may be intimidating, but it is necessary to close the cycle and turn a stranger into a customer and supporter of your brand.

The Sales Pitch. Throughout the chapters of this book, you find many strategies behind creating the most effective sales pitch. Play on similarity, social proof, scarcity, or any other techniques that you have learned so far to pitch your product or service to prospective buyers.

The Call-To-Action. Include CTAs throughout your website (where appropriate) or at the end of emails. Having a button that says "buy now" or "subscribe" may be the final push that turns a reader into a customer. You can learn more about the specifics of a call to action in the book on copywriting.

Follow the AIDA method in the correct order, and you will guide your customers throughout the customer journey until they are active promoters and supporters of your brand. Remember to include all these steps.

40

Mastering Social Media Marketing

Even if you don't know how to write a tweet or know the difference between Snapchat and Instagram, you probably know that social media is key to boosting your marketing ROI and your overall sales.

Social media marketing is on everyone's minds, but how do you make your content stand out among the millions of businesses and people who are posting online every second of the day? Enter Gary Vaynerchuk.

If you're interested in sales, you've probably seen his name. In 2013, he published *Jab, Jab, Jab, Right Hook: How To Tell Your Story in A Noisy Social World*, which includes key insights into the world of selling via social media. Jab, Jab, Jab, Right Hook takes you through the ins and outs of social media strategy. His boxing distinction makes a very important distinction between social media content that sells and social media content that tells your story. The book is worth the whole read, but in this chapter, we'll briefly explain Gary's strategy and how you can use (more) jabs and (less) right hooks to give your customers value and close more sales with your social media content.

First, let's talk about jabs and right hooks. A "jab" is compelling content that tells a story or adds value to your brand. A "right hook" includes a call-to-action and directly asks customers to buy products or move further along the customer journey.

Think of a "jab" as giving something and a "right hook" as asking for something. Gary encourages if you haven't guessed already, three "jabs" before a "right hook." He says, "There is no sale without the story; no knockout without the setup."

Whether you are creating a "jab" or a "right hook," remember that context is just as important as content. Keep it consistent, and make sure your customers can follow the story you are telling from beginning to end (the call to action!)

Consider the platform where you are placing your content. Vaynerchuk includes a guide for what type of content is appropriate for each platform. For example, Facebook is a great place for storytelling, and Instagram is a great place for more creative and artsy posts. Pinterest is amazing for recipes and craftsy tutorials. Different platforms are used for different purposes, so your content should be adjusted appropriately.

One of the most important distinctions Vaynerchuk makes is the difference between distributing content on social media and telling your story. "Jabs" tell a story. Without a proper story, consumers who don't know your products will lose interest, think you're too pushy, or have no reason to engage with your brand. Social media is just that: social. Recent changes to Facebook's algorithm reflect our desire to see live updates from friends and family over advertisements or content from businesses. If you are exclusively using "right hooks," your posts won't appear on your customers' timelines, much less elicit the response you are looking for. The "unfollow" or "unlike" button isn't hard to find.

Keep this quote in mind as you create your "jabs" and tell your story:

Marketers are on social media to sell stuff. Consumers, however, are not. They are there for value.

Offering value includes:

- Product stories.
- Commentary on current events.
- Guides to using your product.
- Tutorials to simple products.
- Anything that was once boring, but you put an entertaining spin to it.

A good story doesn't have to relate directly to your products or to your brand. A tweet or a Facebook post can engage your customers by talking about current events or responding to customer inquiries. Just remember to provide the right context before you share your content!

Let's now talk about that right hook. Too many right hooks turn off customers, but too many jabs don't close a sale. When you are writing "right hooks," make sure they have the following three elements

- A clear and concise call to action.
- The message is communicated and compatible with mobile and desktop devices.
- It is relevant to the social media platform that you put it on (remember that people are more likely to enter their credit card information on a desktop than on mobile).

All the work you have done with your "jabs" will be wasted if the "right hooks" don't do their job.

Vaynerchuk reassures his readers that even if you're not the king of selling on social media, no business is: *"The skill sets it takes to be a successful entrepreneur, a successful marketer, or a relevant celebrity is a different skill set than you needed ten years ago, even though that was the skill set that mattered for decades."*

Mastering social media content and strategy is a top challenge for many entrepreneurs, businesses, and brands. But a few standout campaigns and examples of content show you how you can share a good "jab" of a story.

Humans of New York: Brandon Stanton quit his job in 2010 and started to take photographs of people he saw in New York City as a hobby. Along with each photo, he included a quote from the person; some long, some short, some silly, some emotional, and some powerful. He posted the photos on a Facebook page, Humans of New York. Now, he wasn't looking to sell anything initially, and his content was all the same sort of "jab." But after a few years of posting, Stanton has earned over 18 million likes online, and his "Humans of New York" books have become New York Times bestsellers. People genuinely love stories and love genuinely told stories. Keep this in mind as you showcase your customers or staff and tell the story of your brand.

Vaynerchuk says: "Your story needs to move people's spirits and build their goodwill so that when you finally do ask them to buy from you, they feel like you've given them so much it would be almost rude to refuse." Humans of New York does just that and has used compelling stories and emotional content to sell millions of dollars of merchandise. Basically, you want to give so much value upfront that your customers almost feel guilty for not buying.

41

The Pain of Buying vs. The Pain of Not Buying

Picture this: you're at the checkout at the supermarket, about to put down a lot of money on groceries. You think the bill is too high, and you know that you could get cheaper groceries the next day at a supermarket that has already closed for the night. But then your stomach grumbles. There's nothing in the fridge at home. You hand over your credit card and buy the groceries. In this case, the pain of not buying overruled the pain of buying, and you bought the item.

Avoiding the "pain of not buying" an item is the final brick in the wall for many people who are making big purchases. Salespeople tend to emphasize this pain when they are making their sales pitch, even though there is pain when buying the item, it's nothing compared to the pain of not buying and not having the item. It sounds dramatic, but isn't human nature pretty dramatic already?

Sigmund Freud introduced the **pleasure-pain principle** in 1895. Quite simply, Freud explained that from birth, humans seek out pleasure and seek to avoid pain. That "pleasure" is most often found in the immediate gratification of our basic needs. Humans may make a great effort to avoid immediate pain, even if it lasts for just a moment. (While the "pleasure" side is a more optimistic way to look at human behavior, know that humans are much more motivated by avoiding pain than they are seeking pleasure. This causes Loss Aversion bias.) Let's go deeper.

The pleasure–pain principle applies to things that we both need and want. We buy food to avoid the pain of hunger, a basic human need. If we are in front of a menu of food that can satisfy our needs, our attention is then turned to the food that we want. This is where sales and investments come in. The pleasure–pain principle isn't just triggered by physical needs. Making a purchase can cause the same type of reaction in our brain as obtaining food or shelter. Things get tricky when these purchases make a dent in our wallets. The potential "pleasure" of obtaining an item that we need or want is balanced out by the "pain" of losing money. This idea is central to why people invest in companies that they think will succeed. Letting go of a small bit of money is painful but losing out on a high ROI when the company succeeds is even more painful. Showing customers the "pleasure" and downsizing the "pain" is necessary to close a sale.

If we made our decisions solely seeking pleasure and avoiding pain, the world might erupt into chaos. The following principles and ideas give our actions more structure when seeking pain and pleasure.

The Ego and Reality Principle. Picture a child grabbing food out of someone's hand. The child is looking to avoid the pain of hunger and will do it by any means necessary. This behavior is commonplace for a child but is less acceptable as she or he grows into an adult. As an adult, even if you are famished, grabbing food out of someone's hand is not acceptable. The reality principle stops the person from grabbing food and waits until there is a more acceptable or realistic time to satisfy their hunger. The same idea can be used when making a purchase. Rather than making an impulse purchase to satisfy hunger, thirst, or wanting a new car, the reality principle may kick in and look for a more "realistic" purchase. Tap into the Ego's reasoning when you are talking to customers.

Context and Cost. Studies that look at pain and pleasure in purchases show that the "pain" of a purchase comes from money leaving a customer's wallet. (The evolution of credit cards and digital payments has been shown to decrease this pain.) The amount of pain that comes from making a purchase depends on the context of the purchase and the person making the purchase. A rich businessman may not feel the "pain" of spending $200 on a hotel room, but a teenager without an income may feel pain from spending $200 on anything.

Using pleasure and pain in your marketing and sales pitch sounds easy enough: you want your customers to believe that purchasing will bring pleasure, or at least the pleasure of the purchase will outweigh the "pain" of the price. On the other hand, you want customers to believe that not purchasing the product will bring pain.

- Ask questions that direct your customers to speak on the pain of not having the product or the pleasure of having it. These questions could sound like this: What would having this new car mean to you and your family?
- What could happen if you put this purchase off for a few years?
- How much are you spending on current repairs or increased insurance every month?

These questions give you an insight into what is dictating your customer's pleasure and pain. Steer the conversation in a way that reminds them that the pain of not buying the product outweighs the pain of buying the product.

You can also minimize the pain of buying the product through the following price structures or discounts. A product may offer a limited number of on-sale items or a sale that only lasts for a certain number of days. Having a deadline creates the illusion of pain that might be felt if the customer buys the product after the deadline and must pay the original price. A deadline or a limited number of items gives customers the final push to make an immediate purchase.

Another way to reduce the paying of buying is introducing bundles and packages. Even if your product boasts a lot of customizable features, customers may respond to one packaged price. Adding insurance for one price, safety features for another, and custom detailing for another price increase the chances of your customer thinking they are paying too much for one feature. By packaging all the features up into one bundle, they only have to evaluate one price.

Finally, explore subscriptions and down payments. Making one big payment can sound excruciating, but making a few smaller payments over time? That sounds doable. Monthly or yearly payments sound less painful than one large payment, even if the customer ends up having to pay more in the long run. The pain of not buying the item starts to outweigh the pain of buying the item.

When your customer believes that a purchase is the best way to avoid the pain of not having your product, you will close your sale! Think of it like cracking a safe. Each marketing strategy you use should either decrease the pain of buying or add to the pain of not buying.

42

The Role of Cognitive Biases

When you make a decision, how much of that decision is truly objective?

If you believe that you are purely using logic to assess a situation, you may be neglecting biases that are so ingrained in your mind that you do not notice it is influencing your decision. Cognitive biases shape a lot of the reasoning behind our choices as humans.

Cognitive biases are "mistakes" that influence our decision-making process. These biases are not always harmful but often prevent us from making a truly objective assessment of a situation. A cognitive bias can come from our memories, experiences, or general culture. Many cognitive biases are ingrained in our thought process from the moment we are born. If you can learn to identify these biases, you can take more control over your own decision-making process and better understand and influence the decision-making process of your prospective customers.

In *The Psychology of Human Misjudgment*, businessman Charlie Munger explains how 25 cognitive biases shape us from birth. Some of these biases may seem more obvious than others; for example, Munger explains that humans are "designed" to like and love. We seek out people that we like and love, starting with our mothers. While this bias is not inherently harmful, the like/love tendency can affect the way that we make decisions about people we like or love. If these feelings are already in place, we may ignore traits that would negatively affect our assessment of them.

Other common cognitive biases include

Overconfidence. As we grow and accomplish more in our lives, we become more overconfident in our abilities. Overconfidence can cause humans to make risky decisions.

Confirmation Bias. Once we hold a certain set of beliefs, we are hesitant to listen to information that challenges those beliefs. Many cognitive biases are related to the idea that change takes more effort than we are often willing to undertake. We tend to seek our information that does not challenge our beliefs or encourage any sort of change.

Bias Blind Spot. Until you learn about cognitive biases, you may not notice that they are influencing your decisions. Studies show that people overestimate their abilities to recognize when cognitive biases influence their decisions. To make truly objective decisions, we must consistently address and unpack our cognitive biases.

The relationship between making decisions based on feelings and making decisions based on logic is complex. Feelings and logic are two separate thought processes but can heavily influence each other or completely clash. When we are selling a product, we may be able to logically present the benefits of buying, **but if the customer doesn't feel convinced, then we don't have a deal.** So how do we explain these two separate thought processes and how they work (or don't work) together to influence buyers?

The work of Daniel Kahneman offers a convincing explanation, one that has won him a Nobel Prize. Kahneman is the author of *Thinking, Fast and Slow*. The book separates our decision-making process into two systems, appropriately named System 1 and System 2.

System 1 is the "fast" form of thinking that produces instant decisions based on feelings and immediate reactions. We often don't have much conscious control over these decisions. System 2 is a "slow" form of thinking. When we start to toss around ideas and decisions over and over in our thinking mind, we are employing System 2 thinking. But before we decide to judge and label one form as a lesser form of thinking, we should recognize that System 1 thinking is still based on logic and reason. In the book, Kahneman says that "intuition is nothing more and nothing less than recognition."

Often, decisions and skills that are performed with System 1 thinking are only developed after years of employing System 2 thinking. System 1 and System 2 are separated with different names, but they work together to make decisions. In fact, Kahneman's work shows that when one type of System 2 thinking is employed, other types of System 2 thinking are thrown out the window, giving System 1 thinking a higher chance of being employed. So, what does this mean in the world of sales?

One of the reasons that Kahneman's work has been so revolutionary is the idea that we are making less of our decisions than we may think. This idea applies beyond sales but should be considered when we are pitching our products to customers. In short, **don't give your customers too much to think about.** Even if they are using System 2 thinking to make a decision and weigh the pros and cons of a product, System 1 thinking may beat System 2 thinking to the finish line and make the decision for the customer.

Let's use an example. A customer enters your small store of fishing equipment with the idea of buying a fishing rod. Fortunately (or unfortunately), you have dozens of different fishing rods on display. The number of similar products to choose from is simply overwhelming and requires a lot of thinking to sort out the benefits of each choice.

While the customer is visiting your store, and once you have understood what they are looking for, you might offer a deal on one of two different types of fishing rods. Choosing between the two products requires quick thinking based on intuition and doesn't require the tedious thought of choosing between dozens of options.

As a salesperson, whether you are selling a product or a service, ask yourself how you can employ System 1 thinking to help your customer make a decision. What are the factors that will quickly show your customers the benefit of making a purchase? How can you present your products in a way that the correct option is intuitive?

Even if you have all day to spend with customers talking about a purchase, making a final decision will only take a few seconds. Make those few seconds count by appealing to a System 1 form of thinking.

V

Book 5: The Perfect Business Plan

43

Before Writing a Business Plan

In this chapter, we're going to discuss some steps that you should take before writing a business plan, as well as what it takes to dissect and spend six, seven, and eight hours getting every single detail of your business plan in place.

We are going to cover those two things in this book. Prior to writing up a business plan for this year, let me first show you what's even more important than writing your business plan now.

Many times we will go through a past relationship. And the relationship didn't work. Some of us can't wait to just say "You know what, it didn't work." And we move on, and we go to a bar and meet a new girl.
And we move on.
Then that girl doesn't work.
And then the next one.
And this one doesn't work.
And the next one.
And then this one.
Four years go by. And we say, "Wait a minute. How come I don't have a steady relationship? How come none of these things are working out?" Well, because every single time one of them didn't work, you didn't ask

yourself what you would have done differently. What could you have done differently? What can you change about the next one? Is there a trend that you keep picking up on that you know is not effective, and it's not working for you? We don't do this. In the same exact way that most people write business plans, all they're thinking about is the next year, while the most important data for you is the year that just passed you by.

In order to predict the future, you have to study history.

Here we have an all-inclusive list of aspects that one must consider before writing a business plan.

Before writing your business plan

Step 1: Define your vision.

The moment you start a business, you surely have a clear goal in mind. You know precisely what you wish to achieve with your new enterprise. After some time, however, this vision will become more blurred, and caught by the complexities of running your business, it is possible that you'll forget some of your initial good ideas. Writing down explicitly your vision for the company is a fundamental step. It will help you define the vision itself. Moreover, it will make it easier for your staff to identify with the company's mission. In this way, all the daily activities of the business can be aligned with the stated vision.

Step 2: Set clear goals for the business.

Goals should not be small to accommodate your limitations. Even if you are a new entrepreneur, you should think big and be ambitious. Set goals with different time frames in mind. You will have well-defined short-term goals (to be achieved within a year or so), mid-term goals (to be achieved within three years), and long-term goals (where will your company be ten years from now? Are you planning on an exit? Do you want to expand into other niches/geographical areas? And so on). When setting goals for your business, you should consider all the different aspects. Of course, you should set some clear monetary goals (what is the revenue you want to generate? How much of it will be profit?). But you should also set other targets, such as the number of customers you want to have in your database, which targets the population and age groups you want among your customers, and other specific goals depending on the details of your activity. Don't limit yourself to the financial aspects.

Step 3: Define and write clearly your unique selling proposition.

What is the feature of your business that makes you different from your competitors? Your unique selling point (USP) is what will make you more attractive to potential customers. Why is your product or service different from others in the park? The USP could be anything from providing additional features in your product to personalized customer service. You could even simply offer your audience better after sales warranty and support. Before writing a business plan, make sure you have clearly identified and highlight the perks that your customers are getting from you. The features that make your business stand out among the competition.

Step 4: Study the market you are entering.

It sometimes happens that you have a great business idea, but someone else has already started their enterprise with a similar plan. It is quite a common occurrence, but you must not let this stop you – how many restaurants are out there? Many businesses can provide the same (or similar) service and still survive or even prosper. The marketplace is huge, and it can sustain multiple businesses. In order to navigate such a huge and competitive environment, you should know your market better than your pockets. Research and find out who your closest competitors are, how many of them there are, and what services they offer. Moreover, you should also go more in-depth and investigate the current and future trends of your industry. Know the larger picture -what are the best benchmarks in your niche that you can use to understand and evaluate your business performance, such as gross turnover or profit margins? Once you know the ins and outs of the market you are entering, you can move more comfortably and plan effectively.

Step 5: Know your customer.

This goes without saying - customers are the most important part of a business. Without customers, there is no business at all. Therefore, you should identify precisely the customers your business caters to. Nowadays, people are spoiled for choice. When choosing a product or service, they have thousands upon thousands of options literally. To have any chance that people will even notice your product, let alone buy it, you must have a very precise idea of who your ideal customer is. Before writing a business plan, you must define your target audience and research their habits. Your business won't succeed unless you understand the motivations behind the actions of your customers. Why are they buying? What moves them to take action? When you know the answers to these questions, you can focus on the areas that are of interest to your selected audience and stop wasting energy on the rest. Put yourself in the customers' shoes, and then think about what would make them choose you each and every time. Write down all your thoughts and ideas about this point and implement them.

Step 6: Research the demand.

You have surely studied the demand and supply curves. Is there a great demand for the product or service you plan to offer? You should find out the answer before committing yourself to start the new business you have in mind. The basic rule is that demand must be greater than supply. If this is true in your market, then your business will thrive. However, if the demand is less than the supply, then your business will be in trouble and eventually fail. So, do your homework beforehand and gather as much information as you can about supply and demand in the market you wish to enter.

You can do this sort of research directly online without even leaving your house. Be smart and invest your savings only after having made sure that there is a demand for what you are planning to sell.

Step 7: Set clear marketing goals.

Now that you have finished your research and defined your business vision, what is the next step? You should paint a clear picture of how your product will look like, how much it will cost, and how you will promote and distribute it. Make sure to consider the following four areas carefully:

- Product development strategy
- Price margins
- Delivery methods
- Promotion plans

Step 8: Lay out your marketing strategy.

After setting your marketing goals, you must formulate a plan to achieve them. Here are the questions to consider:

- How many products do you need to manufacture, and at what profit margin in order to get your desired revenue?
- What will be the main strategies and social media you will use to promote your business?
- What will be your system of fulfillment and delivery? What will be your target area?

Be extremely specific when you address these points, as these answers will translate to actions in your business plan.

44

The Business Plan: Executive Summary

The Business Plan

If you're thinking of starting a business, it is crucial that you learn how to write a business plan. Despite starting having a great idea, most businesses are short-lived. Within the first five years of operations, 90% of new businesses fail. Of the remaining 10%, only one of the ten businesses survives after the first five years.

These are the sections that should be included in your business plan:

Executive Summary

In this chapter, you're going to find everything you need to know to write a pro-level executive summary that investors can't help but pay attention to. I'm going to tell you why they are important and what needs to go into them.

Before we start, let's take a little journey. So, imagine walking into a library. You go over to the fiction section. There you find 500 books staring you in the face, begging for your attention. You're going to read them all, right? No, you wouldn't. Instead, you'd find a book that looks interesting, flip it over, read the blurb on the back, and if you're captivated - you'll check it out, leaving the other 499 books to collect dust on the shelf. Well, your executive summary is just as important as that blurb on the back of a 300-page novel. And I'm going to show you how to make sure that YOUR business plan is the one that gets checked out.

Before I give you the steps to writing an executive summary, we should probably talk about why they exist and make sure you understand exactly when it is appropriate to use one. So basically, an executive summary gives an overview of a larger and more substantial document. Usually, you'll find it at the beginning of a document, and it's used to summarize the major points that the document covers. If you've read up on executive summaries online, you'll probably get the sense that they are limited to one single page, but this isn't always the case. Your summary may be longer depending on the length of the document that it is covering. If you turn to the experts, you may get a bit of conflicting information. According to Ashton University, an executive summary should be a maximum of 1-3 pages; but the Miami School of Business recommends a length equal to 5 to 10% of the length of the entire document. Depending upon which philosophy you follow, a 50-page document could have an executive summary with a length of anywhere between one and five pages.

Executive summaries can be used for many purposes, from business proposals to go-to-market strategies and more. But in this chapter, we'll specifically talk about executive summaries in the context of writing a business plan. So you've got your Microsoft Word or Google Docs open, and you've managed to put a title across the top that says "Executive Summary," but now you have no idea what to do. Well, if you want to write the most impactful summary, there are ten things that it should include.

The first thing you want to do in your executive summary is to quickly set the stage by introducing the business opportunity. This means defining what problem exists and proving that there is a gap in the market, creating an opportunity that your team can fulfill. You see, successful businesses aren't the ones that make new fad products or those that get a lot of recognition from the media. Successful long-term businesses are those that solve problems and challenges that affect a substantial number of consumers. Immediately in the first paragraph, you want to lay a strong foundation by convincing readers that a real business opportunity exists.

Next, you should describe how your startup solves these challenges. In other words, what product or service do you offer that makes life easier for your audience? Describe what your product is, how it works, and what makes it better than what the market has available to them already. In this section, you will want to describe the specific features and attributes of your product. And show what makes it special, but you want to do this in the briefest way possible.

The third thing you should explain in your executive summary is your target market. In other words, you should quickly answer these two questions.

First, what particular group of consumers do you target with your product or service? And when answering this question, you want to be able to separate the consumer from the customer and explain both of them if they differ. Take Legos, for instance. Although children are their consumers, parents are their customers. And knowing this, they market towards parents, positioning themselves as a creative outlet with STEM benefits, but they market to children as the "cool toy," knowing that they will beg their parents to buy it. And since the parents are already aware of the educational benefits of the product, it's more likely that they will. And that is how you turn stackable squares into $5 billion a year.

The second question you want to ask is, what are the identifying traits of your market? This includes geographic traits like where they live or work; demographic traits like gender, age, and income level; and psychographic traits such as their internal attitudes or values. And if you've never heard this before, then I hate to be the bearer of bad news, but no business serves everyone. Even if you don't know this yet, investors do. And that's why it's super important that your executive summary explains exactly who was going to buy your product and why. Showing that there is a large market of individuals experiencing a specific problem and that you have a solution to that problem is great. But what investors really want to know is how you make money.

In the next section of your summary, you should detail your business model. In short, a business model describes how your startup delivers value, and it explains how and how much a customer pays. So maybe you have a SaaS startup that uses a freemium or subscription model or a marketplace app that uses a peer-to-peer business model. Or maybe you sell products directly to the end customer using an e-commerce model or retail model. Investors want to know how your business will earn a profit and then how they will earn a return. And their ability to earn a return on their investment is majorly dependent upon your business model. As I mentioned earlier, every business has a target market, and there's something else that every business has as well, and that's competition. And for that reason, the fifth thing that you should explain is your competitive landscape. Now, it isn't enough to just simply acknowledge that competition exists. You should use your executive summary to describe your competitors, explain their position in the market, and detail your startup's competitive advantages. Knowing how you would separate yourself from other competitors is critical. For example, if you're a new social media platform going against a giant like Facebook, the only way you will succeed is if you are providing something that they aren't providing or providing something that they are providing, but providing it better, cheaper, or faster. Angel investors and venture capitalists rarely invest in idea-stage businesses. That's why the next thing your executive summary should mention is traction.

If you're telling investors that your concept is the best one to invest in, then you'll need to show some type of proof. So whether you've pre-registered a hundred users to your mobile app using a landing page or made a hundred thousand dollars in sales through your minimal viable product, you should be able to showcase some type of traction that demonstrates the demand for your product and shows evidence that customers are willing to pay for it. For the most impact, describe what you've done so far and the results of your actions. Once you've explained past traction, then you can focus on upcoming milestones or major activities that you plan to complete over the next several months or over the next year. This timeline will prove to investors that you know what steps you need to take to reach your goals and objectives. Using all the information you've written so far, you should be able to create a believable financial model that showcases the potential of your business.

In the next section of the executive summary, describe your financial projections. In other words, if you're able to meet your sales objectives, how much revenue would the business generate? How much will your expenses total? When will you break even? Use this section to show that your idea is profitable and that you have the research to back it up. But here's a word of caution. Investors want to see promising results, but they want to see real results. So create your financial projections using as much real data as possible. And if assumptions are necessary, then use assumptions that you can back up with data from reliable sources. Outside of the products and services section, arguably, the most important part of the executive summary is the team section. The fact is, bad teams can run a great business right into the ground, and great teams can turn very average ideas into extraordinary businesses.

The team section is the one that readers will focus most of their time on, and if they aren't convinced by this point, then really, the rest is pointless. In this section, express who the founders are, what their backgrounds are, and why their experience is relevant to the business. Many times newer startups haven't fully built their executive teams, and that's okay. But if that's the case, then you at least need to have a strong advisory board that has the experience that your executive team lacks.

Finally, after all of this, you can mention your capital requirement or the amount of money that you're hoping to raise. But don't just add some random number here. Really think about how much you need to take your startup from where it is today and grow it to the next level. Explain why investment is necessary and how the funds will be used. Also used to mention what type of funding you are looking for, whether it's an investment or a loan, and what's your offering a return for the capital, whether that's payback with interest, equity, convertible equity, or something else. So now, you know what goes in your executive summary, but as the old saying goes, it's not really what you say. It's how you say it.

An important part is that it's not just the information that sells. It's the presentation of that information. Because dropping a bunch of words on the page, that's the easy part, but crafting a creative, personal, and impactful document, well, that takes a little more finesse.

The first tip is to write to your audience. Sometimes you may need to write several executive summaries so that you have different ones for different types of readers. Someone who is highly familiar with your industry may know certain terms or phrases, while someone not familiar may become confused with industry jargon. An experienced investor will likely understand certain business concepts that a friend & family investor may not be as comfortable with. Write to the reader in the words that they understand, in a way that excites them and in a way that speaks to their specific goals and objectives. The second tip is to make the first sentence count. First impressions mean everything, and readers will judge the entire document based solely on the first line.

If you can't catch them there, you might not have the opportunity to capture their interest again. Because they simply may stop reading or just do a quick scan over the entire document. When you're writing your executive summary, you have to be purposeful in every paragraph, every sentence, and every word. You want to write in a way that is exciting, persuasive, and compelling, and don't give them a moment to exit. Make it so interesting that they just can't pull away. Also, before you send it over to an investor, have your peers read it over. But don't send it to them over email, have them read it right in front of you so you can see their reaction as they're reading it. Because friends are too nice, and even if it's the most boring thing they've ever read in their entire lives, most of them will tell you that it's great. So look at their body language and analyze their facial expressions as they're reading. If they're gripping onto every word, like the climax of a top-selling novel, then you know that your executive summary is ready.

The final secret is to know your boundaries. Because there's a very thin line between giving too much information and not giving enough information. And you want to provide the optimal amount so that they understand the story without giving away the entire plot. You want to write your executive summary with one goal, and that is to persuade them to read the rest of the document.

So when you write executive summaries, think of movie trailers because a good movie trailer shows you the highlights of the film so that you understand enough about the character, enough about their situation, and enough about the context without telling you the ending. They build you up, and then they leave you with a cliffhanger that makes you desperately want to know how it ends. That's how you create a movie trailer. And that's how you create an executive summary.

45

Company Description

When writing a business plan, the executive summary should be followed by a detailed company description. While in the summary, you touched on the basics, this section should go deeper into the details of your products or services as well as your company structure. In this chapter, we discuss how to write a company description for your business plan. It should include the following:

Company name. This is the official name of your business, registered in the state where it runs its operations.

Type of business structure. It could be LLC, Sole Proprietorship, Partnership, Corporation, Ownership, or Management team. This section should include the names of the key people in the company.

- Location. The address of the company's headquarters
- Company history. This section should tell when the business started, what the company fulfills, and how you got the idea to start it.
- Mission statement. This should be a clear statement representing the purpose of your company.

- Products or services offered, and target market. This is a brief overview of the products you plan to sell and to whom.
- Objectives. This is an outline of what you aim to accomplish in the short term based on the data provided in the rest of the business plan. You can also include more long-term growth goals.
- Vision statement. A statement on how you envision the future of the company.

Do not assume that anyone who will be reading your business plan knows anything about your business. You will need to include a number of specific pieces of information that will help the reader understand exactly how you have set up the business.

A good business description will make your work a lot easier as you travel the road to starting your business. When you write a formal plan with the hope of qualifying for a business loan or attracting investors, you need to let them know that you know what you're doing.

Aside from all of the paperwork and jumping through the hoops others set up for you, the most important reason to write an in-depth business description is to understand who your potential customers are. Your business description must primarily meet the expectations that your customers have when they walk through your doors. Get inside their heads. What do they want? If they're looking for something specific, you can bet there is something else related to it that they want as well. Understand them, offer them what they want, and then break down what it will take to provide it.

The description of your business should leave the reader with a clear understanding of exactly what you have set up, how you not only served others in the past but also how you plan to continue expanding or changing your business in the future. It is, therefore, important that you use clear language and details that will paint a picture in the mind of the reader while also inspiring that person to want to know more about your business because of the interest that they have developed during the reading.

46

Market Analysis and Strategy

In this part of the business plan, we're going to try to identify the market, its size, growth potential, and any kind of trends that might be going on in the market. Typically, there are two different forms of research put into the section:

1. **Primary market research**
2. **Secondary market research**

Primary market research is typically research that you do by yourself. It is specific to your product or service. For instance, that could mean doing a survey and giving it out to people directly to ask them how your specific product and service is doing or giving out samples. It could also mean letting people do test runs or trials, getting comments back, and feedback from the direct market that you're going to be in. It is directly related to your business. This type of research is not as common as secondary market research.

The secondary market research is not specific to your business. If you were to go online and just research your particular industry - trade groups, associations, or government agencies are constantly getting information from industries to see how the economy is going. You can think of a funnel. You're starting out on a wide scale, and you're trying to bring down that scale to your own specific market. We can use bakeries as an example. What are bakeries in general in the U.S. doing? Well, maybe bakeries are increasing by 5% per year now. Why is the trend needed or important? It's because in our financial projections, later on, we're going to include that 5% per year increase, and we will have some information to back up why we think our business is going to grow.

First, we look at the national level, and then we bring it down to a region. For instance, how is our bakery doing in New England? Maybe bakeries are just flatlined, so there are just as many openings as closing. That is an important piece of information. Now, if we narrow it down even further, we will look at what our bakery is doing in Maine. Maybe it is declining. Maybe there are more bakeries closing than there are opening. In that case, that should be your first red flag that maybe you need to relook at this industry to really understand if you are going to be competitive enough in a declining industry. Are you going to have a compelling argument enough to go against that trend if most of them are closing? We are trying to fill our heads with enough information. The more granular, the better.

We're trying to figure out what the size is and what the trends are. By size, we mean two different things.

One of them concerns numbers. For instance, there are so many diabetics in Maine.

The second one relates to how much they are spending and the size of their budget per year. There are x diabetics in Maine, and they spend y on insulin per year. With these two pieces of information, we have a pretty good idea about the size of the market. This is what we need to do in the market and industry analysis section, take the industry in general and try to narrow it down.

47

Organization and Management

If you are writing a business plan for your business, then you will require business management skills to ensure the success of the business venture. There are many business management skills required to successfully run a business, and some of them include proper planning, organization, troubleshooting, and coordination. These core skills are necessary to make the business a profitable and successful venture.

In this chapter, we are going to present your business management skills for writing management and organization in your business plan. Planning is the most important business management skill.

All business ventures have goals and targets, and the only way to achieve them is through proper planning. A part of planning involves predicting the consequences of taking a particular step or measure. Planning involves careful analysis of information in data. This analysis helps the person to make effective decisions. In addition, problems can be handled more efficiently, as planning involves troubleshooting and SWOT analysis. Communication - different situations demand different communication skills. Hence, whether it's negotiation or dealing with a tardy employer, effective communication skills are necessary.

Organizing a business cannot flourish if it is not organized. It is imperative that a person managing a business has good organizational and coordination skills. This will also help keep the workforce focused on the business goals and allow them to work in a harmonious manner.

Financial Management – a business venture cannot be successful without proper financial management. Management of finances ensures that raw materials can be procured, inventory is not too high, and allocation of funds to use different business needs is undertaken. Good methods of financial management can make all the difference between a business venture being successful and unsuccessful.

Inventory – a business should only store inventory that is necessary. If too much inventory is available, it will block the funds which could have been put to better use. When there is inventory, other expenses increase, such as storage security and transportation. All these added expenses have an effect on the overall profitability of the business:

Ethics – without proper ethics, it is not possible to run a successful business in order to survive on a long-term basis. The business should have ethical practices in place. This involves the way business is conducted, how the company handles environmental and other sensitive issues, corporate social responsibility, and how the business handles its workforce. All these factors play a big role in ensuring the success of a business.

The organization and management team of your business plan. This is the part where you're going to dig into and showcase your organization, your management team, and how your human resources team is structured. If you're a Sole Proprietor, of course, this is going to look very small because the management team might be just you. Just because you're a Sole Proprietor doesn't mean that you won't have staff working for you, but if you're just starting out, there might only be you. That could be your management team as well as your entire organization. You could also have managers or staff working for you. If that is the case, in this part of the business plan, you will showcase your team. You should have bios on all of the management team members within your company. It is important to include all the different levels of the organization that you might have. Here are a couple of things to be considered and included:

- If you're planning to hire somebody, whether that be full-time or part-time, to help you with your business.
- If you plan to hire interns or work with a contractor.
- If you're hiring students and plan on applying for grants to help you offset the cost of hiring those students. What their qualifications are, and how long they may have worked with the business.

The organizational structure should be included here as well. For instance, if you've got a president and a Chief Financial Officer. You should also mention if you have a human resources manager. If you own a small business, and there's really just you and a couple of other people, all of those key people need to be mentioned, as well as a little bit about them. The purpose of this piece of your plan is so that everybody gets to know who those key people are within your business. If you have some part-time people or junior employees, you may not name them, as they would soon be replaced by others. You would still need to talk about what their position is and what their key roles are within the business.

48

Products and services

The products and services section of your business plan is probably going to be the longest portion of your business plan. This is where you talk about what your business does and what is the unique offering that you are giving potential clients.

The offering that would make them want your product or services. It could be products, services, or both products and services. In this section, you're describing exactly what it is that your business is doing and what it is going to be known for now. In case you have multiple services or multiple products, you start this section with your largest revenue driver. Primarily, you should write about what business you are, what products or services you are known for, and what generates the most revenue. For example, there might be a restaurant whose primary driver is selling lunch or dinner, and an offshoot would be selling shirts and mugs. You wouldn't want to start with the shirts and mugs because that's not what your business is about. It's about the restaurant and the food. Start with your best foot forward, what you want to be known for, what your unique offering is, and why people are going to want that.

It's very important in this section that you highlight not only your products and services but what price you're going to be offering these for. The reader has to start to get an understanding of where you're going to sit in the market, and this is going to tie in with the competitor section. You're not going to mention competitors at this point. This is the section you're trying to highlight yourself and your own business. One of the hardest things for a business is to try to figure out what price you should offer your products and services for. First, you try to figure out the materials costs, shipping, bottles, labels, and whatever else is involved in a product (e.g., ingredients). Then, you should include the labor cost. When it comes to pricing, there are really three elements involved.

Firstly, a cost model - which is what we just briefly went through - you try to break down all the costs and what you need to make a profit. Then there is the price that competitors are charging. You try to compare that to make sure you price higher or lower, depending on your strategy. Here you should thoroughly analyze why a certain strategy makes more sense for you (i.e., what value do you add so that you can charge more than your competitors). You should ask yourself what is going to draw people to you.

The last thing you have to think about is, "what are my clients going to expect?". You can then justify the price because it's what people would expect from your product or services. The products and services section can be two to three pages long. You should aim not to have your business plan written in the language that a reader who isn't in your industry is not going to understand.

49

Financial projections

In this chapter, you will learn how to create financial projections. Forget memory lane. Let's take a walk into the wild, mystical world of the future. That's right. We're going to see the future... of your business.

A strong financial projection tells you the essentials of where your business is headed. Like how much money you'll make and when you'll make it. Financial projections are key, not just in deciding whether you can afford to go see your favorite band's 2031 reunion tour but also for securing lenders. More than that, financial projections are an important part of any healthy business. They inform you about sales trends, incoming risks, opportunities, and really fundamental stuff like will I be able to pay my employees and cover my bills?

There are two types of forecasts that make a complete financial projection.

One is a sales forecast. How many units of your product or service are you going to sell over the next three years? Also, include how many customers you expect to have and how much profit you'll make.

Two, an expense budget. Make a prediction about any and all expenses over this three-year span. There are going to be fixed costs like paying rent on your office, but also variable costs like marketing campaigns. Don't go crazy here. Just make an educated guess. Okay, that's the pudding. Now it's time for the proof. We need to include financial statements that help give your sales forecast and your expense budget some credibility. These statements contain invaluable information on how your business is actually doing, otherwise known as your actuals. Like flipping over tarot cards, each statement helps build the case for your financial future. Behind card number one is an income statement. It represents growth, desire, and setbacks, and by that, I mean the statement shows your profits and losses to date. Income statements show four elements. Revenues, expenses, gains, and losses. Card number two is a cash flow statement. Concern with the divine fluidity of being and also what you do with your money, cash flow is all about money going into your business, cash in hand, money leaving your business, and cash outlay for bills. Cashflow matters because it shows the most realistic view of how your business is doing. For example, say you've made a ton of sales this month. Yay! But all of your clients haven't gotten around to paying their invoices, and unpaid invoices mean you won't have the cold, hard cash you need to pay your bills. Make sure your cash flow statements cover three things.

One operating activity. These are the daily expenses of running a business.

Two, investing activities. Any investment in your long-term future.

Three, financing activities. Shows any investments from financiers or any payment to shareholders.

The third card is your balance sheet. It's about the balance of assets and liabilities. Make sure your balance sheet shows off three things.

One asset. This is any resource of economic value that you own. This could be cash, inventory, or property.

Two, liability. These are generally debts such as payables and loans. Anything that will cost you money.

Three, owner's equity. After all, liabilities are paid with assets. Any leftover amount is considered owner's equity. Balance sheets are split between assets on one side and liabilities and owner's equity on the other side. The total dollar amount of assets must equal the total dollar of liabilities plus equity. So the formula for an annual balance sheet looks like this: assets equal liabilities plus owner's equity.

So now that you have your three financial statements— cash flow statement, income statement, and your balance sheet— put it all together, and you have an informed sales forecast and expense budget. To be clear, the first time around won't be as easy as making instant coffee, but with a little practice, and you should practice and revise throughout the year, it's totally doable. Last thing I'll say, when creating your projection, be optimistic but realistic. Look around your industry and use your existing knowledge and your actuals to make sure your projections paint a good picture of your business without overstepping. Looks like you're well on your way to creating your first financial projection.

Give yourself a big high five.

You've earned it.

Take action.

If you don't take any action, all your effort in planning will be wasted. Be realistic, and if you find during the formulation of the business plan that your idea isn't viable, don't despair. There are thousands of other opportunities out there, and you can and will ultimately find one that suits you. We have seen how a business plan will provide direction and focus and what is important to include in it. Start your research today, write down carefully all those brilliant business ideas, define your goals, set a viable path to achieving them, and don't let anyone stop you.

VI

Book 6: Fierce Copywriting for Sales

50

What is Copywriting?

If you tell your parents that you just bought a book on "copywriting," they will probably think that it has something to do with intellectual property and legal rights. Like many other people, they would confuse **copywriting** with **copyrighting**. While the terms look and sound similar, there is a massive difference between the two.

Copywriting is the act of writing text with the goal of advertising or other forms of marketing. The product, called *copy*, is written content that aims to increase brand awareness and ultimately persuade a person or group to take a specific action.

Copyrighting is the exclusive right to license, make copies, and otherwise exploit a literary, musical, or artistic work, whether printed, audio, video, etc.

As you can see (and probably already knew when you decided to buy this book), they are two completely different things. But clearing up this common mistake gave us an excellent excuse to offer a precise definition of copywriting.

And why would you want to learn to copywrite? First, you will acquire a precious skill in today's market that can land you a lucrative job in almost no time. But most importantly, if you already have a product or service to sell, writing a compelling copy will allow you to create an automated **money-generating machine** that does the heavy lifting for you. In a sense, your copy is your online salesperson. It works 24 hours a day, seven days a week, without supervision.

Every (good) website you have ever visited, every Facebook ad you have seen, and every piece of advertisement you have stumbled upon in a newspaper or magazine has been written by a copywriter. In fact, **copywriting is an almost $50 BILLION a year industry** where you will find massive demand and relatively little competition. Not to mention that the fees that copywriters ask for are constantly going up at a ridiculous rate. If you become good at writing copy, you can even choose the path of becoming a freelancer instead of using it as a means to sell your products or services. You can easily rake in 6 figures and above a year while being your boss, choosing your clients, and living the "digital nomad" lifestyle. You can write your copy while sipping a cocktail on a beach somewhere in Thailand.

People invest tens of thousands of dollars and many years of their lives to go to college and get a degree just to get a secure job. Being a copywriter is a career path that offers you freedom and financial stability without even the need for a college degree. Copywriters are judged on what they produce, not on their paper qualifications. It is a profession in which practical skills are essential (those that college graduates often lack).

It is, of course, not easy to become a superstar that can charge super high fees, a so-called "A-list copywriter." However, the barriers to entry are almost next to none, and this book gives you everything you need for a solid foundation in copywriting. Our attention is on the practical aspects that will make you attract high-paying customers.

So, if your goal is to pass a marketing exam at university, you should probably stop reading this book right now. But if you want to **learn FAST the best techniques to write fantastic copy**, this is the book for you. You can sign up for a college class where you will overpay for decades-old knowledge that is all theoretical. Or you can read this book that contains all the practical strategies that nobody would teach you in college. Within weeks you could be landing lucrative gigs for various clients all over the globe.

And I am not even kidding. Scores of people get their first projects before even getting to the end of the book! That is the power of copywriting, and this is just the tip of the iceberg. When you dive deeper, you discover that good copy on the website can easily 2X, 3X, or even **10X** a business because of the insane compound effect of something called **"conversion optimization."**

Think about an online business that gets around 1000 unique visitors a month. A certain percentage of these people will buy something, say 1%. Assume that you improve the copy of the website so that it becomes more compelling and persuasive. You could easily raise the percentage of buyers to 2%. That means 1% more. It does not seem much, does it? What is the big deal about it? Well, let us think about it for a second longer. Going from 1% to 2% means that, in essence, you have **doubled your sales**. Only by changing some text on your website! But what if you also increase the percentage of people subscribing to your email list, clicking on your ad, or sharing your blog post by just a few percentage points? Well, things start to snowball, and the little gains begin to have a multiplicative effect. And you will get more subscribers, more likes, more shares, and more paying customers.

"I am not an expert writer, and I suck at English." It sounds like a fair objection. However, the best thing about copywriting is that you do not have to be a literary genius to write effective copy. In fact, you do not even have to have perfect grammar because, at the end of the day, **if you manage to hook people emotionally, they do not really care about some random typos on your website.**

And here we have come to the main point: **the only job of your copy is to move people and convince them to take action emotionally.** Effective persuasion is not about boring facts, true but useless statistics, or clever rational arguments. It is about connecting with your readers' pains, fears, hopes, and dreams so that they feel understood as if you were talking directly to them.

This book is here to arm you with extremely powerful tools to make this happen and move people to take your desired action (and make you tons of money).

This book will give you everything you need for a rock-solid foundation in copywriting, as well as proven tips on leveraging this incredible power in all areas of your life: from growing your business to charming the girl you like and even persuading children to eat those broccolis! These may look like very different goals, but they can all be achieved according to the same principles. You will master those principles once you become familiar with the core concepts of copywriting.

51

How to Write Dangerously Captivating Headlines

Well, just like that. If you are reading this, it probably means that this headline managed to spark your attention. The question we must answer is: Why was it successful? So that we can replicate its effects over and over.

We will answer that question in a minute. But first, let us clear the confusion and clarify the most crucial objective of a headline. Headlines are designed with one thing in mind: **to get the attention of your reader.** This is so incredibly important that we will repeat it once more, with different words:

A headline aims to immediately spark attention and SHOCK people from their zombie-like state!

And I DO mean they have to shock. Why? Are we not exaggerating?

Think about it. When trying to get people's attention, you have to compete with an endless barrage of crazy cat videos, clickbait popups and ads, and millions upon millions of other pieces of content. There is a never-ending stream of media distraction, and you have approximately 2 seconds to get the attention of your reader. After that, it is gone. They will have scrolled past your ad or turned the page, and you have thus forfeited the chance to get your message across.

So how did this headline manage to grab your attention? Let us consider, one at a time, all the elements that work together to make this headline effective.

ELEMENT #1: **"How to…"** This is a classic way to start a headline. It is simple, but **it works.** It works because people are curious animals who naturally want to become better at things. They are intrinsically motivated to gain mastery, just for the fun of it.

"How to" headlines are a safe bet in almost any situation, and you cannot really go wrong with them. They never get old and are used even by pro copywriters.

Sometimes these headlines are so effective that they can last for decades without losing their impact. For example, consider the title of Dale Carnegie's groundbreaking book "How to win friends and influence people."

Think about other ads you must have seen "How to lose 20 pounds in 30 days without giving up on your favorite food." "How to earn with real estate even though you have never invested a penny before." The HOW TO strategy can work, but to hook more sophisticated readers, you need to enhance your message. If you need to step up your game, here is where the next element comes in.

ELEMENT #2: **"Dangerously Captivating"** These are so-called POWER WORDS! They make everything seem visceral, punchier, and emotional. And this is essential! What is the difference between a title like "how to write better headlines" and the actual title of this chapter? It is the emotional impact. We as humans have a limited amount of daily "attention units," and EVERYONE is competing for them. To separate yourself from the noise, you have to use <u>shocking words that hack the evolutionary psychology of the brain itself</u> and **instantly activate systems that were designed by nature to pay attention.**

That is why using **"dangerously"** as an adjective instantly gets attention. It signals a potential threat. However, a much more advanced technique is also being used here. Something borrowed from Neuro-linguistic programming (NLP): "Dangerously Captivating" creates **cognitive dissonance** in the reader's mind. The brain becomes alert in feeling this dissonance and will want to know more to resolve this dissonance as quickly as possible.

Remember, always use emotional power words that get the juices flowing and blood pumping.

The three most powerful words are simple: Free - New - You. While the first one is often not appropriate, you can always find a way to use the other two. The next time a headline captures your attention, stop and analyze the use of power words. Which words automatically cause an emotional reaction?

Some Power Words to Give Your Headlines Extra Punch

Amazing
   Controversial
   Discovery
   Easy
   Effortless
   Guarantee
   How to
   In X easy steps
   Magic
   Mistakes
   Myths
   Powerful

Quick

Remarkable

Revolutionary

Safe

Secret

Sensation

Stunning

ELEMENT #3: **"Like a world-class copywriter"** if you are reading this book, you are obviously interested in copywriting and maybe in becoming a professional copywriter.

So who would not want to become a "world-class copywriter"? Someone successful, in high demand, and who gets compensated accordingly. That is precisely why using this expression works. It leverages an innate tendency that causes people to mimic others who are experts at their craft. It is one of the best and most effective forms of learning since childhood. You want to learn from them, and you also want to become like them.

Notice the power words again: "world-class." Not just "good," not just "great." If you are even slightly interested in writing better headlines, you will probably be interested in learning the secrets to writing headlines like a pro. So it naturally gets your attention.

No acting class promises to turn you into an "average performer." They all pitch their classes with a headline like "Become the next Tom Cruise." It is not hard to understand why. The idea of being the next famous Hollywood star presents itself to the eyes of the reader and evokes powerful emotions. The desires and stakes become high.

ELEMENT #4: **"In as little as 10 minutes"** Most people are lazy or impatient, or both. Nobody wants to waste countless hours learning something new or acquiring a new skill. People are constantly looking for "magic pills," "wonder solutions," "get-rich-quick schemes," and "silver bullets." And when they are not, they want at least a "shortcut."

Again, this is understandable from an evolutionary perspective: we evolved to crave instant gratification and quick cures.

Whether you like it or not, the research on this is detailed: your headline must convey a sense of quickness, easiness, and effortlessness. However, be very careful not to lie about your claim. In this chapter, "10 minutes" works because you CAN write dangerously captivating headlines if you truly implement these tips. However, "How to miraculously earn $100.000 with cryptocurrencies in 2 days" is simply sleazy, and most people will see through it.

ELEMENT #5. Well, in this case, I did not use it in the title. But I could have added another sentence like **"even if you are terrible at English."** This element is used to overcome a potential reader objection and reinforce the headline's message. It is often used in headlines where some benefits are presented to the reader. Here are some examples:

How to lose 20 pounds in 30 days without giving up on your favorite food.

How to earn with real estate even though you have never invested a penny before.

How you can play the guitar in less than two weeks without learning how to read music.

You can start combining the five elements described above (it is not necessary to have all five every time) to create your killer headlines.

"How to" headlines are not the only ones available. We have seen how they exploit the natural tendency of people to want to improve and learn new skills. There is another natural human characteristic that is heavily exploited in headlines. Read the following ones and try to understand which one it is.

80-year-old man has sexual congress 5 times a day

When Mary opened the front door and saw what her children were doing, she could not believe her eyes

Did you guess it?

Yes, it is CURIOSITY: Humans are naturally curious. We want to know more. What are Mary's children doing? What is behind that old man's sexual prowess? We have the itch to investigate. Our attention has been aroused.

What the world's best real estate investors know - that you don't

The ten secrets of the top bodybuilders of all times

Curiosity can also be aroused through **an impossible-to-ignore question.**

Do you also make these unforgivable mistakes in English?

Why are so many people getting rich with [any hot cryptocurrency/NFT]?

Which of these stocks will be the next Google?

Here is an interesting question. How long should a headline be? Research shows that headlines with 10 to 13 words attract twice as much traffic as those under seven words. So, try to find the sweet spot with a headline that is neither too long nor too short.

PRO TIPS

1. **Be specific.** Have a clear image of your audience and write a headline that speaks to them specifically. For instance, How can a stay-at-home mom lose 20 pounds without going to the gym?
2. **Do not start with the headline.** The headline is the culmination of your entire sales message, and it should resonate with it perfectly and harmoniously. Start with the aim of your message (the call to action), and once you have figured out how to get people to your call to action, you have a better understanding of how to grab that initial attention.
3. **Experiment!** Sometimes changing a single word can quadruple your responses. Each word matters when you only have 5-8 words on average to grab attention. Fortunately, headlines are the easiest to test.
4. **Use numbers.** Numbers are a great way to add specificity to a headline. Research shows that odd numbers work better than even numbers.

"When you have written your headline, you have spent eighty cents out of your dollar." — David Ogilvy

52

The Secret to Writing Stunning Bullets

Bullets are a copywriter's biggest secret weapon for killer sales. They are reasonably short, punchy, and targeted sentences designed to pump up emotions in readers. Good bullets resonate with them, eliminate fear or hesitation, and reinforce the buying decision, even when people are on the fence.

Powerful bullets take regular facts concerning your product and make them exciting for the prospective customer.

Why write bullets at all? Because people love them! In a world where attention is at a premium, they are short, sweet, and easy to read. Some of the most effective ads of all time are just a headline and bullets.

Research has shown that writings with at least one bulleted list every 500 words get 70% more traffic than content without bullets.

How do you write bullets that will genuinely impact your audience? Well, here is the crazy-effective four-step formula that the pros use to write exceptional bullets.

STEP #1: List the Features. Start by listing out all the features attached to your product or service. By features, I mean whatever relevant characteristic of your product and whatever it can do. Features can be related to physical or technical elements of the product, observable aspects, size, or shape. But if you sell a service, the features can just be all the different aspects of your offer. Do not neglect anything. This list of features will be the starting point for creating the bullets.

STEP #2: Extract the Benefits. Next, you must "translate" these features into actual benefits that personally affect your customers or improve their lives. For example, a benefit might be something that tastes good, gives satisfaction, allows fast and easy results, saves time or money, makes money, or allows peace of mind. People must personally identify with these benefits.

Let us be honest: nobody except you cares about the features of your product. People only care about how the features translate into a concrete (and immediate) benefit in their own life.

Feature: "This book will teach you to write better." Benefit: "So you can write effective copy, triple your conversion rate and make more money." Sometimes it is a bit hard to figure out what is a feature and what is a benefit, but in this case, always ask yourself, "So what?". "These shoes glow in the dark"...So what?... "So your kid can feel like a true badass." You see the difference? The critical thing to remember is that good bullets overwhelm your prospect with the value you give them. Your prospective customer should not have to 'figure out' why something is important to them. Instead, you must TELL them clearly and boldly.

STEP #3: Enhance the Benefits. Here is the point where you will insert some spice when presenting the benefits. Applying the techniques described here will help keep your customers engaged and make your message more effective, thus 10X your conversion rate.

1. Power Words. Yes, the same class of words we discussed when talking about headlines. Those that evoke an immediate emotional response. They are used to pump up energy and keep the reader engaged. For instance, instead of "Get more customers," you could say, "Get TONS of new loyal customers!" Remember that people DO NOT want to sit and read your ad. They are busy going about their lives. You must keep them fully engaged in your sales message.

2. Authority. A touch of authority always adds to the strength of your message. You can build up your authority (for instance, mentioning relevant scientific studies or statistics, which will show the reader that you know what you are talking about). You can also exploit someone else's authority. "The 30-minute training used by Hollywood stars to build the physique of a Greek God".

3. Surprise. Add an element of surprise, a counterintuitive twist to make things even more compelling. For instance, "How to deep clean your closet WITHOUT removing your clothes." People will think, "Really?" and keep reading to satisfy their curiosity.

4. Deal with Objections. Since this is a book on copywriting for sales, I am assuming that the goal of your copy is to sell your product or service. Bullets are the best place to pre-emptively answer potential objections concisely and decisively. Since they touch on emotional hot points, they easily strip readers of their fear, increasing your conversions by a massive amount.

The main objection of a potential customer is always, "Will the product work?." One effective way to deal with this is to let your previous customers speak. You should quote them directly. One or two positive testimonials that resonate with your audience can reassure your prospective buyers that your product is effective.

STEP #4: Complete the bullets. It is time to assemble all the elements considered above and write some striking bullets. Remember, the goal is to take something that is TRUE and gives real value to your prospect, and then communicate it in a BOLD way to trigger critical emotions. Bullets are a place where you can tease, whisper, shout, create intrigue, and even shock! Do not worry about crossing the line. This is the one place where you can certainly do it (but you still have to stay truthful). And you can write different types of bullets (at least 5-6) because you never know which one hits the nail on the head, which one makes the reader say, "OK, this is perfect for me. I want it NOW!"

Another thing to consider is using visual elements to highlight certain emotions. Use things such as:

- (Parentheses) to mimic whispering.
- *Italics* to emphasize a single word.
- Underlines to make sure people do not miss a critical line.
- **Bold** & CAPS to mimic shouting.

EXAMPLES

Now that you know the basics of writing stunning bullets, you can have fun looking for examples online. Just type on Google the name of John Carlton, the undisputed king of bullets (also called the "most ripped-off copywriter of all time"). You will find plenty of high-quality bullets to inspire you. Bullets which, if you are the "right market" for them, will have you salivating and dying to know what is coming. Here are some of John Carlton's best:

- How to pull off unwanted body fat by the pound while keeping muscle loss to an absolute minimum! (Most "experts" will tell you this is impossible, yet Leo did it without a problem! And he will show you how to do it, too!)

· The 7-step formula that even an illiterate drop-out can use to write advertising copy 100 times more potent than the BEST Madison Avenue ad agency!

· "Insider" tips from the world's savviest (and richest) businessmen on how to shortcut your way to obscene riches and success!

· How to avoid the dumb things 9 out of every 10 people do in business that almost guarantee they will fail miserably!

· How to use the other "dirty" street-fighting tool not allowed in any civilized boxing or karate match because of its immediate ability to disorientate and topple your opponent! (It also works when you do it incorrectly!)

53

What Master Novelists Can Teach You

Everyone loves a great story. Stop and think about the last time you were captured by a book, a movie, a newspaper article, or even a post on Facebook.

Chances are that an exciting story hooked you. And it is no surprise at all! We evolved to be extremely sensitive to stories, mainly because these were the primary vehicles of information humans had for thousands of years.

Our ancestors would gather around the fire and exchange their experiences in narrative form. Being sensitive to stories meant absorbing more information, thus increasing the chances of survival.

The most compelling stories, those that were remembered and passed on through the generations, were those that evoked powerful emotions: fear, love, greed, curiosity, lust, or hatred.

The power of stories to hook and move people is well-known in copywriting and in marketing in general. If you can tell a great story, people WILL listen to and connect with you.

Stories are a great way to gain credibility, highlight elements of your personal struggle, and establish instant rapport (which is extremely important for selling).

<u>Establishing rapport</u> means initiating some sort of "relationship" with your audience. A relationship that allows communication to flow naturally and effortlessly. How do you establish a connection if you are not even there in person to talk to the potential customer, who is simply browsing your website or reading your ad?

You have to TELL A GREAT STORY.

Every story is based on three simple elements:

1. Setting up the problem. For instance, by describing how your life was at one stage. This is usually the "negative" part of the story. Remember that you want to hook your audience, and people are generally more receptive to struggles and difficulties.

2. Achieving epiphany through action. In this part, you must tell what you did to solve the problem.

3. Resolution. What your life looks like after the struggle is over.

Think about the last novel you read or the last movie you watched. I am sure that, in some way, the characters went through a similar arc: struggles - action - resolution. It is the so-called *"hero's journey,"* a timeless archetype for stories, legends, and myths that can be found in every culture around the world. The reason why it is so omnipresent is that it is closely tied to the experience of every human being. Each and every person can relate to a story of suffering and difficulties and rejoice at the overcoming of those issues.

Here are three popular story types based on the "hero's journey" model. They all work exceptionally well in copywriting:

Rags to riches

Stories about someone who went from being a nobody to being extremely successful against all odds. This story type works well because we are all fascinated by life-changing transformations, and we secretly wish we could achieve the same feat. Another variation of this story type is the victory of the underdog, the "David vs. Goliath" story. Such a story captures us since we naturally identify with and root for the smaller guy.

Been there, done that

This type of story works really well when you have a large dose of experience in something that your audience is interested in. You can use such a story to emotionally connect with your prospect's pain and instantly show them that you deeply understand what they are going through and can truly help them.

Great discovery/revelation

We are all familiar with this type of story. The seller tells us how they discovered a "secret formula," a "blueprint," a "framework," or "cracked the code" about a complex problem that we are also dealing with. Even though most people are skeptical about reading things on the internet, you can immediately grab their attention with such a story, especially if it seems unreal!

Use stories as wake-up calls to bring readers out of a passive state and put them in an active state, primed and ready for your offer.

Most people are full of problems. They go about their daily life, but their mind is constantly thinking about their personal issues. If you want to capture people's attention to deliver your sales pitch, all you have to do is select a relevant problem, emphasize it, and then offer a solution. It sounds really simple.

However, people get easily distracted and will be looking for ANY objections to leave your web page or stop reading your ad. The way you will prevent this is by <u>keeping them hooked with a story</u> that they simply cannot give up in the middle. They will NEED to know how it all ends. And you will tell them the end, but at a small price: they will have to stay and read your sales message.

We have seen the importance of storytelling and some templates for captivating stories. But how can you write them in a compelling way? Here are some tips:

- Consider the great examples of storytelling that you have witnessed in your life. Take your favorite movies, your favorite novels, and your favorite TV entertainers. Ask yourself what triggered your interest. What can you learn from these examples?
- Every story should be written with passion. Remember that you are trying to hook the reader emotionally. Your mantra should be "I shall not bore the reader."
- Practice storytelling with family and friends and study their reactions.
- Use lots of verbs and visceral words to add emotional depth and dynamic to your narrative.
- If you are telling a personal story, be genuine. Do not be afraid to show your vulnerability.
- Edit over and over. Nobody gets it right the first time. The best writers are those that edit mercilessly.
- Start your story with an outrageous twist, then dial it back to credible levels.
- Get deep and emotional, and highlight the human aspects of the story!
- Do not mention boring facts, stats, or numbers (these will come after

you have hooked your prospects emotionally). At this stage, you are trying to create an emotional connection with them, not lecture them.

54

A Foolproof Technique to Connect with Your Readers

When writing copy, you should not write whatever comes to your mind. You should not even have to "invent" or "guess" what to write about. Instead, if you have clearly identified your target audience, there will be little guessing to do. You should just use **the same words, expressions, and general lingo** your customers use. Adopt a style and language that is guaranteed to resonate with them.

In this chapter, I will show you exactly why using your customer's language is one of the best things you can do to maximize conversions and how you can do it without any hassle.

In case you forgot, copywriting aims to convince your readers to take the action you want them to take. To do this, you need to connect with them emotionally and resonate with their pains, fears, hopes, and dreams. One of the best ways of achieving this is by speaking directly to them in their way. Do not use generic words and expressions, but genuinely inject your voice into the conversation that is already happening inside their heads.

Research has demonstrated time and time again that you cannot simply coerce someone to take an action. At least not for a long time and in a systematic manner. Therefore, your best chance of success in persuasion is to use your audience's internal motivation systems. You should present your argument in a way that seems like it originated not from you but from inside their heads. That way, you can **minimize their feelings of "being sold to"** and maximize their willingness to take the action you want them to.

What you should aim for is to write as if you were only speaking to a single person in a highly personalized way. This is the so-called *Rule of One.*

Let us face it, **people love to feel special and crave extra attention.** *The Rule of One* works incredibly well because it touches on these concepts and transforms the reader from being indifferent to becoming highly susceptible to your sales message. The rule works well on its own, but how do you know who should be your "One"? How do you choose the correct tone of voice from the thousands of people who visit your website or read your ad?

This is where customer research comes in. I know what you are thinking: "Arrrgggh, do I have to waste time with tiresome customer research? Can I not just make up what I want to say?" You could do this, but your results would be hit or miss. I know it is a nuisance, but the only real way to find out with certainty how your customers speak and what they say is to observe them in places where they hang out and listen to them. This is by far the best way to ensure you nail your sales message. Do you want **"quick fixes"** or **conversions**? Fortunately, nowadays, doing the necessary customer research is not so hard anymore, and you have a plethora of options for getting the most crucial information:

- You can engage in a genuine 1-on-1 conversation with a few of your customers.
- You can monitor the comments on your latest post and make notes about

exciting themes.
- You can ask people to reply to your emails saying that you personally read each response.
- You can create surveys of various complexity and collect honest feedback.
- You can ask a few people to get on the phone with you.
- You can even "meet them where they are" by joining live events where your typical customers hang out. For example, if you are in the men's dating niche, you can go to the pubs and clubs where these guys hang out and see if you can discover any trends in their behavior or attitudes.

Sure, doing these things takes "going the extra mile." However, this is precisely what will differentiate you from your sales competitors and "wannabe copywriters." Almost nobody does this under a certain skill level, and their copy suffers as a result.

What if you are introverted and shy, and the **last** thing you want to do is to talk to your customers? Are you doomed to fail? Not necessarily. I will now share with you an advanced strategy that allows you to get the most out of customer research without actually speaking to them directly.

Keep in mind, however, that ultimately there is no real substitute for genuine 1-on-1 conversations. But this is the next best thing. Fortunately, technology allows us to gather a significant amount of extremely valuable information pretty quickly and entirely for free.

Here is what you should do:

1. **Think about your niche.** Then write down your target audience, what problems you solve, and what separates you from anyone else.
2. **Create a customer avatar.** Create a detailed description of your ideal

customer as if he/she was a real person. Take your time with this task, and ensure you define every little detail as precisely as possible. How old is he/she? What is his/her job? And so on.

3. **List objections and hopes.** Based on the information above, list three of your ideal customer's pains, hopes, and dreams, as well as fears and barriers that prevent them from buying.

4. Excellent! Now comes the fun part. **Browse online** for people with similar problems on social media channels. Here are some great channel suggestions as a starting point:

Quora - Try to brainstorm questions that relate to your avatar's problems.

Reddit - This is a goldmine for listening to the voice of your customers. Plenty of great conversations are happening all at once, and people are very open to sharing their deepest fears and desires.

Facebook groups - Find five groups where your target audience likes to spend their time and browse through the comments. You will be surprised by all the great insights.

1. **Take notes. LOTS of notes.** Tens of pages of notes! And then distill the best parts into hooks, benefits, and even headlines that you could use in your copy. Once you get the hang of it, this process becomes quite enjoyable. And the results will speak for themselves.

Congratulations! You are now better than 90% of aspiring copywriters out there.

55

Make it Painful for Customers Not to Buy Your Product

There is an interesting phenomenon that we have all experienced many times in our life.

Your partner goes away for a few days, and suddenly you miss sharing your meals with him/her. It is a freezing cold winter day, and you are missing the warmth of summer. But by the time summer has arrived, you think longingly of winter. We all know the underlying principle of what is happening: We desire more strongly something that is not readily available.

In behavioral psychology, this is called the principle of **scarcity**. It applies to both business and life in general. Whatever is scarce is highly desired. On the contrary, whatever is available in ample supply (and it is not directly linked to your needs) gets devalued and discounted.

So how do you solve this problem when trying to sell your products or services? Well, you **introduce scarcity**. But customers are not that naive. Claiming fake scarcity will not work. You must operate with REAL, genuine scarcity.

Something that can be taken away from your prospects if they do not act now.

Something that will make them feel like a fool if they miss it.

Something that has the power to invoke the need for instant gratification now.

Real scarcity creates turbulence and cranks up people's greed through the stratosphere! It plants such a powerful seed in their heads that they will not be able to sleep until this "conflict" is resolved.

And here is the master's stroke: When they are feeling the pressure, you give them even more reasons to act. You add exclusive bonuses, special offers, the opportunity to become a part of something great, and other great benefits.

There are two concurring forces you are leveraging here.

1. Use scarcity to increase the pain associated with NOT taking action that is, with not buying your product.
2. Use bonuses to lower the pain associated with spending money on your product. Anything that makes them feel unique, privileged, smart, or lucky IF they take action NOW.

You will win the customer if their fear of missing out outweighs the pain experienced in parting with their money.

Let us examine a few ways to integrate scarcity in an intelligent manner in your sales messages. Every strategy is presented with a concise example. Remember that the goal is to create an aching urgency to take action.

Quick-action exclusive bonuses

This premium bonus is ONLY available to people who know what they want and take action right now, before the end of this webinar.

One-time offers

I have officially gone crazy and decided to give away this absurdly rich package for a true pittance. My spouse has already threatened to divorce me for this, so it will definitely not happen again.

Limited discounts (use them carefully, or you risk devaluing your brand)

At the bottom of this email, you will find a code that will allow you to get a **50% discount** on your order. This code is only valid for 24 hours after opening this email. Hence the clock has already started to tick. Grab it now, or miss out!

Limitation on the number of products/bonuses available

There are only 20 seats available for this event, and 12 are already booked. I honestly cannot guarantee how long it will be before all seats are taken, so I suggest you reserve your spot right now!

Price goes up later contrasted with huge benefits today

Once the doors close, I have no idea when we will reopen them again. And the price will probably go up, too. If you sign up now, you will get **lifetime access**, including all future updates, at no charge.

Fear of losing your spot

The invitation in this email is a special privilege reserved ONLY for people like you on our "Hot List." This exclusive invitation means that you have earned a spot on that list, so there is a special offer here for you. If you do not want it, do nothing. We will take your name off the package and send it to the person below you on the list instead.

Playing on Ego/potential disqualification

This product may be too powerful for you. Not everyone can handle the extreme body transformation this system is capable of.

Fear of losing access

You better hurry and secure access to this course before it is taken down forever. There is a lot of great content in it. In fact, it contains the exact techniques I teach in my 1-on-1 coaching. My clients will NOT be happy to learn how inexpensively I am making this material available. So, frankly, I am not sure how much longer I can reasonably keep this course available at such a low price!

The elite group opportunity

We are only accepting a certain number of new subscribers this year, and we are rapidly approaching our limit. You might have to wait until next year before we onboard new members.

Bonus for a limited number of buyers

The first 50 people who buy will also get 1 hour of 1-on-1 coaching with me, absolutely FREE.

Good news/bad news

The good news is that there has not been a better time to market information products online. The bad news is that our program is so incredibly popular that we now require a paid signup fee for the once-in-lifetime opportunity offered by our webinars. This way, we can weed out the serious people from the tire kickers.

Take inspiration from all these examples to implement scarcity in your copy and get people to TAKE IMMEDIATE ACTION.

WARNING: Be very careful because people are not stupid. If they find out that your "one-time discount" is just a ploy, and you "tricked" them, you will lose them for good (and your reputation will suffer too).

Be honest yet bold, using scarcity in an ethical way, and you will achieve massive success!

56

The Single Most Influential Element of Your Copy

What is the most important part of any sales message? Naturally, it is the Call to Action (CTA). In a sense, everything leads up to this point, and every single persuasion element is designed to increase the chance of people clicking your CTA. But why is a CTA important? Can you not simply assume people will act on their own if you did a good job persuading them? The answer is No. You have to specifically tell your leads what you want them to do and why it is good for them.

Based on the type of copy you are creating, the level of detail associated with the CTA will vary.

Let us consider the example of a simple landing page. For those who do not know it yet, this is a web page that has been created specifically for marketing purposes. In this case, the best CTA consists of a short text that resonates with your headline and is **benefit driven** from the point of view of your prospect.

According to the tone and style of the page, your call to action might read:

"Get instant access now!"

"Start your free trial today!"

"Yes! I want to start my journey towards a healthier and more satisfying life NOW."

"Hell yeah. Send me [product X] NOW!"

Take a few minutes to think about what you will write on your CTA button. Research has shown that many visitors do not click if the prompt on the button is too generic. The first simple way to increase by over 200% the conversion rate of your CTA is to make it **personal**. Choose words that make that simple action of clicking on that button valuable and personable to your customer. If you have researched your target audience carefully, you will know what words resonate with them and will move them to take action.

When instead of a simple landing page, you have at your disposal a complete sales page or an email, then there is more room to "warm up" people for your CTA button. In this case, you should present the same CTA several times throughout your sales page, each time accompanied by various hooks. This way, you can intercept people at the right moment, whenever they are ready to comply with what you are asking them to do.

Here are all the places where you should place your CTA in an email or a sales page.

Right at the start

This call to action will capture your hardcore fans or the highly motivated leads that, for some reason, do not care about your message. They just want to buy straight away! It may be because they know you already or for some other reason. In any case, it is wise to put a CTA at the very beginning so that there is no risk of their enthusiasm being extinguished along the way.

Immediately after your offer

Right after you have presented your offer, drop a CTA. This is for people ready to buy directly after seeing your product.

Right after testimonials

As every marketer knows, social proofing sells. What better time to ask for the sale than right after presenting some convincing success stories?

At the very end

Do not forget that many prospects tend to simply scroll to the end of a page to see what is there. You do not want these people to miss seeing a call to action. Also, if someone reads your entire message and you hit them with a CTA at the end, there is a good chance they will make a purchase.

Keep these strategies in mind also if you are producing sales videos.

Now that you know when to use CTAs let us look at the four critical steps that lead up to a high-converting CTA on a sales page. Each step builds on the one before.

Step 1: Tweak your prospects' emotions. Remember that people **buy based on emotion and then justify their decision with logic**. So the first step is to speak to them on an emotional level to make them CRAVE your product.

Step 2: You have to reinforce the rational reasons why your product is such a good investment. How will your prospects explain spending money on your product to their spouse? How can they brag about their life-changing purchase to their friends? You have to give them a concrete reason why buying your product is a wise choice.

Step 3: Create a detailed "Here is what to do now" section. This is a critical part and is often overlooked. You must be direct and precise. People tend to underestimate how straightforward one has to be with warmed-up prospects. It is best to simply lay out everything in front of them:

- Exactly where they have to click.
- What message they will see.
- How to enter their payment information.
- How much time this process will take them.
- When will they receive the product.
- What to expect at each step.

Step 4: Add a P.S. section with additional ideas, reminders, or reinforcing messages. This is the perfect place to mention your rock-solid money-back guarantee one more time.

Or you could remind them that the clock is ticking and the exclusive bonus/discount will soon disappear, so if they do not want to miss out on this opportunity, they should act now. Or you can help your prospects see, touch, and feel what their life will be like once they have your product. You can even include a so-called *binary close* to contrast their lives with and without your product. Here is an example.

"Are you not sick and tired of spending your energy and money on useless [Type of Product], wasting years in the process and with not much to show for it? You can do nothing and keep struggling, or you could change your life today with a proven system that holds your hand every step of the way and just works. The clock is ticking. What are you going to do?"

At this point, if you successfully communicated your sales message, gave your prospects real value and a great story, and answered all their objections and insecurities, they WILL BUY from you.

One last note. Make sure that in your CTA, you are triggering people's "instant gratification" module. **Convince them to act right now!** Not in an hour, not tomorrow, not after reading anything else. Right now! There are thousands of reasons why you could lose even the best prospects if you let them off the hook, so do not risk it. At this point, you have to mercilessly convince them that they must drop everything and do what is right without wasting any more time. That is the way to close the sale for good.

As we have seen in this chapter, a CTA button does not perform magic on its own. It is a critical piece of the puzzle but needs a proper setup to work effectively.

The call to action is the "coup de grâce," the final push that instructs people to buy. It must bear the promise of a better life and be expressed clearly, boldly, and directly. Think carefully about the wording of your call to action and make it as personal as possible. But avoid what most people do, simply slapping cheesy text on a button and expecting miracles. Employing the setup explained in this chapter is the real key to boosting the effectiveness of your call to action.

57

What Every Online Marketer Does

We are talking about landing pages, of course, possibly the most confusing critical element in all of copywriting.

First, let us try and understand what we are talking about. Landing pages are NOT home pages and are certainly NOT regular web pages.

A landing page is a standalone web page where a visitor "lands" when they have clicked on an ad or something similar. Landing pages are designed with a single focused objective known as a Call to Action (CTA). Notice that each landing page has a SINGLE goal, just one! As we will see below, this is extremely important.

People (including many marketers and web designers) think that a landing page has to look "cool," have a "wow factor," or "be clever." Nothing more wrong! Instead, what we need to build an effective landing page is so-called *conversion copywriting*, a particular type of copy that focuses very heavily on customer research, data analytics, and scientific persuasion techniques.

To have an excellent landing page, you need survey data, know the actual language of your customers (including the exact words they use), and perform A/B testing of alternative versions constantly. Do you feel like you do not have time for all this? Well, there are some powerful hacks that few people know about and can make up for 90% of the lack of customer research. Despite being so important, these concepts need the least time, money, and energy to implement. They can be summarized in the so-called **Rule of One**.

The Rule of One consists of four points that you should constantly keep in mind when writing a landing page:

- You write as if you were talking to a single reader (your ideal customer).
- You only try to communicate a single big idea (so that your message is crystal clear).
- You only paint the picture of a single promise (but create maximum impact with that).
- You only present them with a single offer (only one type of call to action).

If you do these four things right, you will create a better landing page than most "professional" online marketers.

How can you easily implement the Rule of One? A great way is always to **write copy only targeted to the 20-35% of your traffic** that is most likely to be part of your ideal market.

The people in this fraction of traffic should be identifiable with your customer avatar, that is, a fictitious individual who is the most representa-tive example of your market. The great thing about writing to your avatar is that you can be sure that your message creates **a powerful emotional impact**. It will not influence everyone, but it WILL influence those who count the most, those who will become your raving fans, spread the word about you, and become repeat customers for life!

Now that you know about the Rule of One and are on track to nailing your messaging, it is time to gauge the awareness level of the reader.

You must remember that not everyone will be attuned to your message in the same way.

There are five stages of awareness that you must distinguish:

1. **Unaware.** When they have not yet identified their pain or your role as a solution to that pain.
2. **Pain Aware.** When they are feeling pain but have not yet recognized that solutions exist for that pain.
3. **Solution Aware.** When they have felt the pain and discovered that solutions exist for it.
4. **Product Aware.** When they know your solution is one of the solutions to their pain.
5. **Most Aware.** When they know your solution is one of the solutions and it is likely to be the best solution to their pain.

Why is it so important to gauge the level of awareness of your readers (or, better, the 20-35% of them to whom you will speak)? Because your approach and your messages must be completely different based on your avatar's awareness stage.

If your avatar is *unaware*, you should help them identify their pain (see the next chapter on this point). If your prospects are *pain aware*, you should help them discover a soothing solution to their burning pain. If they are *solution aware*, you must have a solid **Unique Selling Proposition** and explain why you are better than the competitors offering alternative solutions to the same pain. If they are *product aware*, you can start giving them compelling reasons to buy your product (like using scarcity tactics). Finally, *most aware* people simply need the last push. A promotion would do the trick nicely.

Design your landing page so that it only speaks to the level of awareness of your avatar. Doing so will give you better conversion rates than 80% of landing pages that just randomly toss out text that "sounds good."

Here are a few additional points to remember when you are creating your high-converting landing page:

- Your landing page is often the first point of contact between you and your prospects. Make it count!
- You are selling prospects a better version of themselves, an ideal life, something they CRAVE.
- The best way to persuade is to join the conversation already happening in their heads. Therefore, write in a personal style aimed at a single person that can resonate with the readers.
- Nobody cares about you or your product or service. Everyone who gets to your landing page will ask, "what is in it for me?" So write everything from the reader's point of view.
- You cannot appeal to everyone. Focus on having the maximum possible impact on your avatar customer.
- Your language has to be short and to the point, touching pain points and painting dreams.
- Be clear and specific so that people will understand your message.
- Write at around a 9th-grade level.

The bottom line is, **do not create copy that "looks good," but create copy that converts!**

58

A Wickedly Effective Copywriting Technique

What you are about to read is one of the most powerful tools in copywriting to make your prospects say, "shut up and take my money." It is a curious strategy; at first, it may even seem a little counterintuitive. The truth is that it works wonders, and nothing compares to its raw emotional power. It is called **agitating the problem**, and it will change how you look at persuasion forever.

Why in the world should you AGITATE your prospects' problems? Should you not cure their problem and help to soothe the pain instead? No.

And here is why:

People want to avoid losing more than they want to gain something. We evolved to be highly susceptible to fear and potential losses. Thousands of years ago, we did not have modern cities, healthcare, medicine, or abundant food sources. If our ancestors made critical mistakes, they most likely paid for them with their lives. There were usually no second chances.

For example, it was much more evolutionarily adaptive to be cautious when finding some new colorful berry than immediately eating it for a few calories. It was just too much risk.

The same was true for snakes, spiders, heights, and even social interactions. Upsetting the tribe could get someone expelled from the group, which usually did not end well.

Therefore, our decision-making system evolved to be extra sensitive to being cautious and fearful, and psychologists even coined the term "loss aversion" for this phenomenon.

FEAR is the most primal human motivator. Terms such as "aversion" or "loss" are closely linked to this fear. That is precisely why agitating the problem works so well.

It is simply not enough to rationally state what your prospect is most likely afraid of. He/she knows that already. The issue is that **they do not really care enough to do something about it**.

Deep within their heads, the problem is not real enough. It is not something that warrants an **immediate cure**. Therefore, your job as a copywriter is to *make* this problem very, very *real.* So real that it comes alive and starts to torment your prospect where it hurts the most.

It is like twisting the dagger for maximum pain and inducing a state of personal hell in the reader unless they take action by accepting the hassle-free, easy, and quick solution. You offer them your solution to immediately dispel this heavy feeling and lift them to their heaven.

So, how do you agitate the problem? You make everything emotional, visceral, and volatile. People have only a vague idea of their problem until you agitate it. They have no idea how big it is. So, according to Jon Benson, one of the best video sales letter copywriters out there, **"Your job is to tell**

them everything that could go wrong when this problem remains in their lives."

At this point, you start explaining the ramifications of living with that problem in great length and detail and with emotion. You can speak to their anger, resentment, guilt, and even embarrassment. If you do this right, your readers should be *terrified* of this problem, and the only thing rushing through their minds should be, "Oh my god, this has to stop! I cannot let this happen! What should I do? If only there were an answer!" And at that precise moment, as a knight in shining armor, you ride into their battlefield and offer a solution capable of quickly saving them. And they will be craving it at this point (though that does not mean they will immediately buy from you just yet!).

It is well known that if you want your hot dog stand to be successful, you do not need a great location, competitive prices, or tasty food. All this becomes secondary when you have a **starving crowd** coming your way. *Agitating the problem* does precisely that for you. It creates a hunger in your audience. And you will be there ready to feed them.

Is it not much better to have people craving your solution than half-asleep couch potatoes who just say "hmm" when they read your copy? Agitating the problem is a wonderful way to zap people out of disbelief mode and make them instantly connect with you on a deep emotional level.

Now you know how vital this emotional hooking is for successful persuasion. In fact, it is *everything.* Without it, your copy falls flat. There is no connection or impact, your prospect is not moved, and most importantly, there is no selling. Yet so many marketers forget about this crucial step, and they just list four questions that identify the problem and immediately offer up their solution. Do not do this. It is simply not a good way to sell. There is a reason why every successful sales letter has a nightmare story. It is all about agitating the problem.

However, one more thing is critical to nail this part. Make sure to agitate the **right** problem! Because you could be the best copywriter in history and still completely miss the mark if you agitate a problem that your audience does not care about. And I am not talking about things such as highlighting the pain of growing orchids to internet marketers. I am talking about the serious, non-superficial problems that are *really* preventing your prospects from happiness. For example:

- People do not just want to lose weight. They want to feel good about themselves.
- People do not want to simply become rich. They want the lifestyle that wealth allows.
- People do not buy a convertible for speed. They buy it to impress the ladies and look fabulous.

So, how do you find the right problem to agitate?

As mentioned in a previous chapter, you do it by researching what your customers want. You have to find out what your market is talking about in their day-to-day lives in places such as online forums, Facebook groups, Reddit, or Quora.

Alternatively, you can speak to people directly and find out using open-ended questions. A good one you can use is "What is important to you about X?" It is the only way to discover the burning problem, for sure.

For instance, the conversation could go like this.

- "I want to lose weight."
- "What is important to you about losing weight?" Answer: "I want to

look good in the pictures."

- "What is important to you about looking good in pictures?" Answer: "I want to get compliments from people."
- "What is important to you about getting compliments?" Answer: "Then I would feel really good about myself."

BINGO!

Now you have their **real** burning problem, and you can safely go ahead and **agitate it like a boss**.

59

How to Effortlessly Close Your Sales

If you have read this far into the book, you know a surprising amount about high-converting copywriting by now. Throughout these chapters, one theme covertly permeated every topic and silently contributed to the success of these techniques. It is time to spell it out.

The concept we are talking about was popularized in the famous "Stanford marshmallow experiment." That study showed children's natural tendency towards **instant gratification.**

The interesting aspect about all animals, including humans, is that when the chance to gain something valuable presents itself, we want it instantly. We want it **now**! It is hardwired into our brains. Giving up a sure but small reward often needs some serious cognitive abilities.

You do not have to be a child to be affected by the mechanism of instant gratification. Even as adults, we simply hate waiting for rewards: for muscles to grow, for fat to be burned, or for money to accumulate. Like it or not, people do not look for prevention, hard work, and delayed rewards. They want **"instant cures," "magic pills,"** and **"quick results."** In fact, they wanted these things yesterday!

Even if you think that your target market is somehow different, that they are all sophisticated intellectuals, the same rule still applies. People will generally choose instant gratification over delayed rewards any day of the week. Sure, some possess an extreme amount of willpower and are hyper-rational, but what are the chances of you having an audience made up mainly of that type of people? Slim to non-existent. Therefore, do not take any chances, especially when you can use persuasion techniques that leverage the incredible power of instant gratification.

Here we explore a few of these techniques:

1.Use power words and strong verbs.

When writing anything, you want to avoid sounding plain and boring at all costs. One of the best ways to ensure that your copy has a powerful effect is to replace plain words with fierce words. For example, instead of "increase," you could say "supercharge." Instead of "better," you could say "remarkable," and instead of "cool," "bloody amazing." See the difference? This is a good start. However, you can take things up a notch by frequently integrating benefit-focused words in front of your verbs or in front of any significant word. The benefit of this is twofold. First, it makes the text more compelling. Second, it "tricks" the critical-thinking brain area into focusing no longer on analyzing the crucial word itself but on the validity of the preceding benefit-focused word.

Here is an example to illustrate this point:

"Get more customers" —> "Instantly gain a ridiculous amount of loyal customers."

The underlined words elevate the emotional impact of this statement and reinforce its value, jacking up the **'must-have emotional need'** of the sales message.

2.Use greed-inducing bonuses tied to a condition.

What gets the juices flowing more than jaw-dropping bonuses? Many copywriters love rewards so much that they make it seem as if they are more valuable than the main product. However, you cannot just have random bonuses lying around and expect people to shower you with their money. You have to give them a solid reason to act immediately and receive tons of free stuff or hesitate and risk losing all that valuable extra stuff forever.

That is why people use the "unexpected bonus," the "first ten buyers to get...", the "early bird pricing," and the "fast-action webinar-only price." The aim is to create a sense that the prospect is making a bargain, thus making an already good offer irresistible.

This strategy works exceptionally well because it directly contrasts all the benefits and instant gratification you can effortlessly get within a few minutes with the fear of missing out and losing everything. In other words, it makes **the pain of NOT buying bigger than the pain of buying**. And it works like a charm.

3.Remove every last bit of friction with your close.

You have to understand that even if you have delivered a perfect sales message, people will still be on the fence and look for any tiny reason NOT to buy from you. And as the age-old sales saying goes, "If you let 'em slip, you've pretty much lost 'em." This is why you have to finish strong and make it as easy as possible for your prospect to start enjoying the incredible benefits of your product, not a week from now, not tomorrow, and not even today, but RIGHT NOW! This is why you frequently see expressions such as "get it now," "immediate delivery," "same-day shipping," "yours today," "own it now," or "call right away."

It turns out that when deciding whether to make a purchase, one of the major influences in our decision is how fast we can have the product or service. And this makes sense. You went through all that trouble to grab your prospects' attention, hook them emotionally, present them with a strong offer, list tons of excellent benefits, and give them every reason in the book to buy now. At this point, if they are still reading your message, they are **salivating** for your product, and they want it badly. But there is still that little voice inside their heads that says, "Stop! Do I really need this?" Your job is to silence that voice and start talking about your product as if your customer owns it already!

At this point, you do not say, "If you buy this, you will get this and that." You say, "When you get instant access to X, you can immediately start applying the life-changing techniques found inside." You must make them feel like they do not have to wait anymore. In this way, they do not lose that built-up desire. Instead, they get everything right now. Heck, they can feel the taste of ownership already! That is how you leverage the incredible power of instant gratification and close way more sales.

60

Change This One Thing in Your Copy

Let us play a little game. I will provide you with two short paragraphs of the same text. Then, you decide which one sounds more interesting to you.

Okay, here it goes.

Version 1

"In this guide, I would like to talk about personal pronouns because I think they are essential in copywriting, and I have used them to great effect whenever I had to write something persuasive."

Version 2

"In this guide, you will learn about personal pronouns because, as you will see, they are essential in copywriting, and you could use them to great effect whenever you have to write something persuasive."

Wow! What just happened there? I will tell you exactly what happened. You probably already forgot about "Version 1" because it did not give you any compelling reason to retain the information. You probably thought, "Okay," and skimmed over it.

But chances are that after reading "Version 2", your eyes lit up, and you thought, "Hmm, interesting, tell me more about it." So, why was "Version 2" more persuasive?

As you probably already have guessed, **it focused on YOU instead of ME.**

The brutally honest fact of life is that in business, especially in an online business, nobody really cares about you. People only care about themselves. People only care about you when they are trying to figure out if you can help them solve a problem or give them something they want. Even storytelling, which technically talks about you, is only effective when your personal story is **relatable to your audience.** When it has a lesson or moral that is also applicable to them!

I know it sounds harsh, and many people would object to this, but it is just a fact of life. Now, this does not mean that people are shallow or egotistical. It only means that if you want to grab their attention online, you should talk about them and never about yourself. When you have to talk about yourself, highlight how you can help them.

This is so incredibly important to your copywriting success that you should write this down somewhere as a personal mantra. **It is not about you. It is about them!** If you spark their attention by talking about something that could be of personal interest to them, they listen. If not, they phase out.

Especially in today's world of never-ending media distraction, there is always a funny cat video lurking behind the corner, waiting to steal your reader's attention. The best defense against this is to keep your reader's attention engaged and speak to them in a personal tone. It should feel like a natural conversation between you and them. Think about it like trying to insert your voice into the conversation that is already happening inside your prospect's head.

At first, you just connect slowly and carefully. But, eventually, if you are doing a good job, you will start to blur the lines between their thoughts and your message. Remember, the ultimate goal of copywriting is to move people toward taking the desired action. The only way they will reliably do that is if they **feel like it is their idea** and they are intrinsically motivated.

Getting to this state is not easy. However, by using a lot of personal pronouns (**"you"**), you can eventually blur the line between what you are saying and what they are thinking.

Remember to constantly talk about your reader in the second person, using the pronoun "You" liberally to achieve this. The more you use "you," the better. There has been much research proving that higher use of this pronoun correlates with a more successful copy.

"So that means I should use a bunch of "you" pronouns everywhere? What about "we?" Good question! Do not use "we." Seriously, do not use it! Many companies and people use "we" instead of "I." Nevertheless, the same applies to both of them. Remember your mantra, "**It is not about you. It is about them.**" Your visitors do not want to hear about your organization, team, achievements, or pet tarantula (Okay, maybe the pet tarantula is cool!). They want to hear about themselves, their problems, their needs and wants, and how they can create a better future for themselves.

The **only** case when you should use "we" is when you say, "we promise." That is right. You can use "we" when it is still about the readers, when it lowers their pains and fears, for instance.

Here is one more thing to consider. People do not trust you, especially online. There are so many scammers and spammers on the internet that people have put their guard up.

In fact, according to the Harvard Business Review, "If you are running a business, this is what you contend with: the rampant assumption that your main goal in life is to part fools from their money."

So, why should they believe you when you talk about yourself or your team? You could simply make all that up.

Sure, you could make up false claims and promises as well. However, emotionally connecting with your readers, you inevitably gain their trust, even if they have trust issues.

To recap, one of the most certain ways to gain your readers' trust is by talking to them in the second person, using many "yous." If you want to talk about yourself as well, fine. But here is how you should pull it off: use the first and second person together to create a conversation between you and your reader. Talking one-on-one with your reader creates a **feeling of intimacy** and mutual exchange.

Here is another popular expression to keep in mind when you want to create copy with a feeling of dialogue with your readers: **"write as you talk."**

Compelling copy keeps your readers front and center. They may want to know more about you or your product, but their main concern is themselves. Therefore, even when you share information about your story or product, always stress how it affects the reader.

Remember, it is not about you. It is about them.

61

Readers Will Devour Your Content

Think about your favorite Netflix series. Do you not get pissed sometimes when an episode ends with a huge cliffhanger? Well, you are not alone, my friend. This also grinds my gears big time. Yet it works wonders for the creators of the show. Why? Because this cliffhanger gives you a very strong reason to keep that TV show at the top of your mind and painfully count the days of the week until the next episode, where everything is revealed (hopefully).

In today's world of information overload, we are constantly bombarded with an unbearable amount of new stuff, each item fiercely competing for your attention, which is surprisingly limited.

In fact, research has shown that we each have a set amount of "attention units" per day, and these get depleted as we are exposed to new information. Have you ever felt like shopping in a huge mall or supermarket is extremely tiring mentally? That is because there are so many messages and subliminal cues competing for your attention that you simply get overwhelmed.

Typically, you quickly forget about anything you see or read, but there is a catch. There is something that directly hacks the psychology of the mind. An ancient technique that is probably as old as advertising itself.

It is a surprisingly potent, mind-bending super-tool that has the power to glue the attention of your reader or viewer to the screen.

Do you see what I just did there? Right, I was teasing the heck out of this topic: **information gaps**. If you have read this far, you have seen for yourself why it is so effective.

So what exactly are information gaps, and how should you use them?

Information gaps are psychological triggers you can use intentionally and strategically to hook your prospects' attention and keep them excited about what you are saying.

They work because humans tend to **seek a sense of closure**, not to let things be incomplete or open. Everyone wants to get to the end of a problem or story. Marketers and behavioral psychologists have long realized how to exploit this innate tendency of ours to sell more.

Here are three specific ways to incorporate information gaps in your copy.

1. Curiosity

This is another human trait that goes back thousands (or even millions) of years and is deeply entrenched in our psychology: we are innately curious creatures. Just look at children and how they tend to examine everything about the world around them.

Even though our parents eventually teach us to have some restraint, this internal motivation still stays with us until the end. Probably the best place to leverage the power of curiosity is in the headlines.

Blogs, YouTube videos, Facebook ads, sales pages, and emails all use curiosity-based headlines to great effect.

For example:

- *"The amazing health secret of the oldest person in the world"* to pitch a supplement.

- *"From 1975-1980, what single investment appreciated approximately 450% more than bonds... 398% higher than stocks... 175% more than houses and 74% more than diamonds?"* for an investment opportunity.

Believe it or not, these headlines are several decades old, yet they still work wonders.

Curiosity is timeless, and if you manage to come up with something that you KNOW is of great **interest to your prospects**, something that touches on a pain point, highlights a fear, or provides a glimpse of a better future, you KNOW they are going to read it.

Be careful not to go overboard with this. Everyone hates clickbait headlines, and even though you might pull this off a few times, people will quickly realize that you are a phony. Make sure you understand the difference between clickbait and genuine curiosity.

2. Open Loops

These are the equivalents of cliffhangers in TV series. It is a technique where you tease something that you are going to discuss or which is about to follow logically. However, instead of talking about it immediately, you digress and start talking about something else.

All you have to say to implement this technique is: "I will talk more about it in just a moment, but first, let me properly introduce myself," "I will tell you exactly how I did it in a minute, yet first, I want to let you in on a little secret," "Before I tell you what X is and what makes it so unique, let me first tell you what it is not."

Use a few open loops in each piece of content, and people will read or watch more of it. It is as simple as that.

3. Building Anticipation

Last but not least, this version of the curiosity gap is best used before trying to pitch something. In fact, pro marketers often have sophisticated anticipation email sequences before product launches to "warm up" prospects and create buzz around the launch. Huge companies often spend millions on these campaigns, but here is how you can achieve the same effect for free.

Create a simple, 3-5 part email campaign before launching something, and share valuable content with your readers. However, the catch is that at the end of each email, you add an open loop that directly teases the next email and keeps it at the top of your prospect's mind. This way, when you send the next email, they will be waiting for it! The same as you with the next episode of your favorite show.

All you have to do is to include a P.S. at the end of each email with something like: "In tomorrow's email, I will show you a step-by-step guide on how to X so that you can Y... Be sure to keep an eye out for it!" Then in the following email, the first paragraph links to this P.S. That is it.

If you do this, you will no doubt see your open rates soar, and people will be waiting for your emails.

62

The Three Magic Words

If you have been reading this book up to this point, you probably noticed that it talks a lot about **benefits**.

But what is so special about benefits? Why should people not be persuaded by features just as much? It turns out that when you are writing copy, you have to assume that your audience is just like a bag of potatoes. It may sound harsh, but in today's never-ending age of media distraction, people have become incredibly low-focus.

You have just 2-3 seconds (!) to make an impact and to get their attention with your headline. Then you have to work really hard to hook them emotionally with a story. Even when you finally get to your offer, you could still lose them in a blink of an eye UNLESS you fuel their desire with **mouth-watering benefits**. Keep the benefits in plain sight at all times, and your reader will be hooked. Because everybody always wants to know: "What is in it for me?"

We have already seen this, but it is worth repeating the concept because I know that you will immediately forget about it when you sit down to write your copy.

The moment you are there with your hands on the keyboard, and you feel the urge to start describing in detail the excellent characteristics of your product, and highlight all the cool features and next-level specifications, just STOP! Take a deep breath and try to accept the unfortunate truth. Which is that nobody cares about these things. Why?

Because people are egotistical and they want to get something from you, especially on the internet, ideally for FREE. Instead of a lot of statistics, numbers, and boring details, you must convincingly show them **what these features can do for them** in their own day-to-day lives!

Show the benefits from the readers' perspective, touching their pain points and catering to their hopes and dreams.

Nobody wakes up in the morning and dreams about the specifications of their coffee machine, but they DO dream about that fresh, tasty cup of coffee in the morning!

Now that we have clarified the concept let us introduce the **magic words** that allow you to turn features into benefits smoothly. You should ALWAYS use them in your copy because their power is almost unlimited.

Without further ado, here they are:

"SO THAT" // "AND THAT MEANS. "

Here are examples of how to use them:

This computer has 16 Gigs of dual-channel ddr4 memory **so that** you do not experience any lag.

This vacuum cleaner has a 2000 Kwh motor **and that means** that you can quickly and effectively get done with the cleaning.

This course is jam-packed with over 40 hours of video and over 1000 pages of content **so that** you have everything you need to become a master in X.

This phone's battery capacity is 4000mah **so that** you do not have to worry about charging your battery for 48 hours.

This food is low in polyunsaturated OMEGA 6 fats, **which means** it is better for your heart.

Do you see the power of the magic words?

Notice that we are not ONLY using benefits and totally skipping features. That would sound unprofessional. Moreover, there are plenty of cases where eye-catching features are selling points of their own, and this depends on the niche.

For example, a computer nerd will be salivating over a video card with 2800 CUDA cores, but to most people, it means nothing. A nutrition expert will be all over the macronutrient composition of food, while others just care if it is healthy and tasty.

The best course of action is, of course, to COMBINE features and benefits. **Always use both.** If you remember the three magic words, combining features and benefits becomes astonishingly simple and can be divided into three steps.

Step 1

List out ALL of the features of your product or service. Everything you can think of, such as contents, physical dimensions, weight, color, and smell (if it has any). Everything that comes to your mind. Write all of this down.

Step 2

Brainstorm potential uses <u>for each and every feature</u>:

How can they make life easier?

How can they make things cheaper, better, more convenient, and less risky?

What feelings, fuzzy emotions, or satisfying sensations can these features evoke?

Anything that makes people FEEL better. It can relate to their emotional, physical, or financial life.

Remember that we all make decisions primarily based on emotions, so it is better to directly **address emotions** in a sales message. Constantly ask yourself *in what ways your prospect would FEEL better if it were to have your product or service.*

By the way, keep in mind that a single feature can have multiple and diverse benefits.

Step 3

It is time to <u>use the magic words</u> to create eye-popping copy that includes the features of your products and immediately explains their benefits.

Using this 3-step recipe, it becomes ridiculously easy to create a TON of bullets and make your offer **jam-packed with value.**

The best part about this approach is that you never know which benefit connects with a particular person. Many times people will join for a single benefit!

In case you are still struggling with confusing the features and benefits, here is a great way to figure out which is which; just keep saying *"And that means"* until everything makes perfect sense.

Here is an example.

This chapter teaches you about the features and benefits

and that means you will become a better copywriter

and that means you will make more money

and that means you will be financially independent

and that means you will not worry about money, and you will enjoy life more and be happier.

Here we go. Now it makes perfect sense. You got to the **core feelings** you want to touch on with your benefits.

Remember that, more often than not, people do not even know what they want and what makes them happy. That is why you have to approach the problem from several angles and see what sticks.

It is usually best to just **OVERWHELM your prospect with the massive value** provided by your benefits. Do it in a way that your prospect does not have to "figure out" why something is important to them. Instead, you TELL them in no uncertain terms, with vivid details, and in an emotional way.

Make sure to always focus on benefits, and you will see incredible results.

63

How to Write Killer Emails

First, you have to differentiate between "cold" and "warm" emails because they have totally different strategies.

Cold Emails

These are sent to people who do not know you and who probably have never heard of your brand. Although cold emailing is a great lead generation tool, it has many problems, for example:

- You often get automatically flagged as spam without people actually reading your email
- Your email deliverability is far lower than if you had an email list
- It is VERY hard to sell something to people with a cold email directly
- Even in consulting, it might take 3-5 follow-up emails to get quality engagements

However, if you can write in a fun style, come up with an intriguing subject line, and spark some curiosity, you might have a shot. This is true both for B2C and B2B. Also, your success will depend heavily on how you segment your list. Segmentation means that you know what people on your list are interested in so that you can custom-tailor the email to their needs, wants, fears, and dreams.

We now describe a few best practices to increase your success with cold emails.

First, let us talk about subject lines.

Remember that the subject line has only one job: get the email to be opened. You do not need to convince anyone of anything with that line. It will not be opened if it sounds too much like a promotional email. You should create subject lines that are informal and spark curiosity. Here are some techniques to do that.

The confusing subject line

White wine and screaming children

Why I paid this guy 4k for a few hours

The straight-on-the-problem subject line

Are you still struggling to lose weight?

(Address the problem, not the solution)

The news-related subject line

Use the language of your audience and make subtle references to current events that your target audience is very likely aware of / following.

Examples

This happens as often as a royal wedding

The World Cup of stock traders

The counterintuitive/controversial subject line

To spark interest with this kind of subject line, you really need to know your audience. Cold emails can truly work, but you must shoot at a very well-defined target.

Why this so-called "safe stock" is a bad investment

Why do I grow my muscles without drinking protein shakes?

The pun subject line

Think and grow broke

All quiet on the crypto front

Now let us get down to the actual email content. Make your messages short (around 100-200 words) and extremely easy to read. Do not talk much about yourself. Get your target interested in how you can help THEM from their point of view.

When you write a cold email, your goal should be to get the recipient to take a specific action (e.g., subscribe to your newsletter). You do not want the reader to give up reading after the first sentence. Since it can be difficult to find the right points to persuade someone to do something, we will now provide you with **the framework that will guarantee that your email is crisp**

and relevant.

AIDA

Attention

The first part of your email should get the attention of the reader. This is a catchy sentence that does not allow them to take their eyes away. In the cold email copy, this is your subject line. The trick here is to make it relevant to your customer. Relevance is the key to smoothly transitioning from *Attention* to *Interest* in your email.

Interest

At this stage, you have to pique their interest. This is one of the most challenging parts of your email copy. It is essential to stay relevant to your target audience. The best way to get them interested by telling them precise results they could achieve if they took one particular action, for instance.

Desire

This is when your readers will crave what you are presenting to them. They should now think to themselves, "I have to buy this!" or "I am subscribing to this newsletter!" If you have a Unique Selling Proposition, this is when you get to emphasize it. Link your USP to the needs of your reader, and tell them how they could benefit from it. Another way the desire could be triggered is by showing them a *short* testimonial of one of your customers with great results. Make them want to be in their shoes.

Action

Congratulations! You have now managed to keep their interest until the last step. This is where you clearly and concisely tell them which action they should take. Do not be vague. Your prospects want to be told what they have to do. They do not want to have to guess. This part can be tricky. Here is what will make the difference between success and failure at this stage. You must not ask for a huge commitment. You do not want to get them to set up a sales call. They do not know you yet. They will take the action you want them to as long as you make it simple and easy for them to do it.

Now that you have this framework, you only have to keep these four stages in mind when writing your email. You will not get distracted by adding irrelevant facts that your readers do not care about. Keep it concise and to the point.

After you hit send, make sure you follow up several times after a few days, it is normal for people to ignore you for days.

"Warm" emails

Although cold emails have their place in the world, the real money maker is having an email list of your own and regularly giving them valuable content (insights, tips, tricks, hacks, bite-sized techniques, etc.). This way, you have an unprecedented opportunity to build a genuine relationship with your audience, which is extremely important in today's "sleazy" marketing world.

The best way to transform your leads into paying customers is to give them real value most of the time and only **ask for the sale in 10-20% of your emails**. First, you give, and then they will pay happily.

Moreover, if your contacts know that they can expect actual good content from you (and not just constant sales pitches), your open rates will be much higher (you can expect between 50-70%), and your click-through rates will at least double.

Let us see the best practices to follow to create an effective email campaign.

- Email amazing content frequently and regularly (at the very least once a week, but it is best if it is twice or three times per week).
- It does not really matter if your emails are long or short. Just send something valuable.
- Constantly test different subject lines and CTA buttons to find out what works.
- Always remember your ultimate goal: Building a relationship with your readers.
- Send four engagement emails for every sales email. This will make the latter very powerful.
- Always write in a personal tone that sounds like a genuine conversation.
- Do not worry if people unsubscribe from your list. You only want to keep engaging with the "right" people.

By keeping these simple best practices in mind, you will already be ahead of most online business owners.

Let us see how a simple but very effective email funnel can help you launch a new product. You write six emails in total, and every email has a single goal. Use the following structure:

Email #1

Introduce and expand your idea while giving them some valuable tips.

Email #2

Get your readers excited or engaged, and agitate their problems.

Email #3

Offer a real solution to their problems and introduce your product (still no hard sell).

Email #4

Highlight the value of your product with case studies, testimonials, or a great story.

Email #5

Answer common questions and objections that might prevent people from buying.

Email #6

Increase urgency and implement scarcity the smart way to get readers to take action.

Do you see how easy that was? Now you have a powerful funnel that is simple and works extremely well.

It is not necessary to overcomplicate things. Usually, 5-7 emails are enough. You only need dozens of emails when you are selling a high-ticket course ($997+).

As for the length of individual emails, generally, 300 to 700 words will work just fine, but it depends on your audience and how many stories you are using. You are using stories, right? If not, start using them left and right because stories are your most powerful weapon when it comes to engagements.

If you can create a narrative with drama, a protagonist, and an antagonist, people will actually look forward to your emails and pay close attention. In fact, the narrative of your email is even more important than its design. People care more about the emotional experience rather than a good-looking design.

If you implement the tips in this chapter, your success with email marketing will immediately skyrocket, no doubt about it!

Just remember: always, always **keep giving value**, even while selling. Push people to make a decision that is in their best interest, and they will love you for it. Even if they do not buy, they will feel that they have learned something, and next time they WILL buy.

64

The Lies Your Customers Always Tell You

When interacting with your leads and investigating your target audience, make sure you are aware of the difference between what people say and what people actually do.

We all like to appear more cultured than we actually are. When you ask questions about media consumption, for instance, people tend to lie. Try and ask people on the street what their favorite website is. How many people will answer YouTube, Instagram, or Facebook? Yet, those are the websites where people spend most of their time online.

Or you can try and ask people about their favorite author. How many will mention E. L. James or some other writer of erotic fiction? Yet those are the best-selling books on Amazon.

Here is another example. Very few people will admit to getting their news from BuzzFeed. Yet, the BuzzFeed website has more traffic than any other mainstream newspaper.

Why is BuzzFeed so popular (and so are YouTube, Instagram, etc.)? Because they focus on entertainment. All the most watched TV shows are entertainment-based rather than info-based. Look at the list of the highest-grossing movies of all time. You will see the first spots taken by the Star Wars movies, the Avengers movies, and the Harry Potter movies. That is pure **entertainment**.

The bottom line is that if you want to understand your customers, then you must consider where they spend their money and time rather than listen to what they tell you because it is always difficult to admit our constant need for entertainment.

If you want to make money, you must be entertaining. This does not mean that you should be clowning around. That is only one way of being entertaining, but it does not always work. Here are some other strategies to make your copy entertaining:

- **Stories**. We have already stressed the importance of implementing narration in your sales pages, and we have devoted a full chapter to the best narration strategies.
- **Controversies.** People are attracted to controversial topics. Whatever product or service you are promoting, I am sure you can find plenty of hot gossip in your niche. One of the best ways to entertain using controversy is to use the formula "[Celebrity in this niche] says X. Here is why he is wrong."
- **Listicles.** These are articles structured as lists. Things like "The Top 10 Thriller on Netflix in November 2022". They are the most read type of articles on the web. Implementing listicles in your copy (especially in your email campaigns) is an excellent way to inform and entertain.
- **Quizzes.** You will be surprised by how effective they are. Something super simple like "What type of [product in your niche] are you?" can get a TON of traffic. People love quizzes and find them entertaining. They are also one of the best lead-generation tools. You can have people answer 6 to 8 questions and then have them enter their email to receive the result and find out what type of vacuum cleaner they are. Since they have already invested time in completing the quiz, they will likely

comply with your request.

The take-home message: be entertaining, and your copy will stand a much better chance of doing its job.

65

Putting Everything Together: How to Sell a Vision

This is the most effective persuasion method ever employed. It has been used by royalty, religious leaders, and the world's leading companies and is also present in books and movies. We are talking about the power of a **vision**.

You can overcome all your customers' objections if you inspire them with a vision. Better still, you should depict two contrasting visions.

The Positive Vision:

"Think about what your life could be in 20 years if you start building your investment portfolio now. You will be able to retire, enjoy more time with your family, and travel to any place in the world."

Dive deep into the details, and make a vivid depiction of the **customer's dream outcome**. If you do this right and they believe you, they will want your product no matter the price.

The Negative Vision:

"Jim never cared about financial planning. Despite a successful corporate career, now all he has is debt, a house worth half of what he paid for it, and a daughter he cannot afford to send to college. The financial difficulties have also strained the relationship with his wife, who is filing for divorce."

The most powerful emotion we experience is FEAR. When we are afraid, we are more likely to take action to make that emotion disappear. If you depict a vivid horror story, your prospects will be moved to act immediately.

How do you create a vision? One potent tool is **metaphors**. Metaphors carry a built-in vision. They make the concept you are describing alive and immediate.

Consider the following line by John Carlton, written to advertise a product in the golf niche.

Your drives will soar through the air like missiles.

You can see and hear that ball flying, right? Here are some other examples of the power of metaphors.

If you don't use these tax breaks, the government will take your money like candies from a baby.

FBI-like profiling techniques to get inside the heads of your customers.

Another technique that can enhance the presentation of your vision is called **future pacing**. You bring your prospect into a hypothetical future and have them consider how they would act in that scenario. The magic word here is IMAGINE.

Imagine knowing how to develop an immune system so powerful that it can even fight cancer.

Your product will not cure cancer. But it can be part of a vision where people take better care of themselves and build more muscular bodies that are less prone to get sick.

Starting with the sentence above will immediately captivate the target audience of your product, let us say people in their sixties whose primary concern is being in good health and finding out how to live longer.

Here are some other examples of future pacing.

Imagine knowing the exact three words to say to a cold call prospect which guarantee they will at least hear your pitch.

Imagine being part of a secret "Supper Club" of investors who receive the most cutting-edge biotech knowledge before even Wall Street gets ahold of it.

Of course, your product will not do **that**. This is a hypothetical, creative scenario. But the use of imagination will enhance your vision and stay in the mind of your readers.

We have come almost to the end of the book.

Before saying goodbye, let us stress once more one of the core concepts of copywriting: Always **focus on the benefits for the readers.**

Praise the VALUE you are giving the customer, and describe the significant results they will get. Emphasize the contrast between the high value received and the small effort and commitment needed on their part.

The small $50 investment you are making on [Product X] could [return $10.000 or more/make you lose 25+ pounds in 8 weeks…].

All it takes to [Big benefit] is [small commitment].

You want to make the price seem inconsequential, a pittance, compared to what you are offering. One great strategy to achieve this goal is making a comparison with commonly used products.

For instance, if a subscription to your service costs $49 a year, you could say

$49 a year means just giving up on a cup of coffee every other week.

We discuss at length in this book how to overcome the readers' objections. Questions like

- Is it possible?
- Is it beneficial to me?
- Can anyone do it?
- Can I do it?
- What is different from all the times I have failed in the past?
- Why should I act right now?
- Will this violate my moral/ethical code?

Which of these questions is the most important for your audience?

It depends. You will have to do your research and find out. It depends on the level of awareness of your prospects (see earlier chapters). Address that most pressing objection first, and you will close your sales in the blink of an eye.